ARTS AND MINES

Always great to
meet great teachers
and glad you are
Still enjoying my
art

[illegible] 5/93.

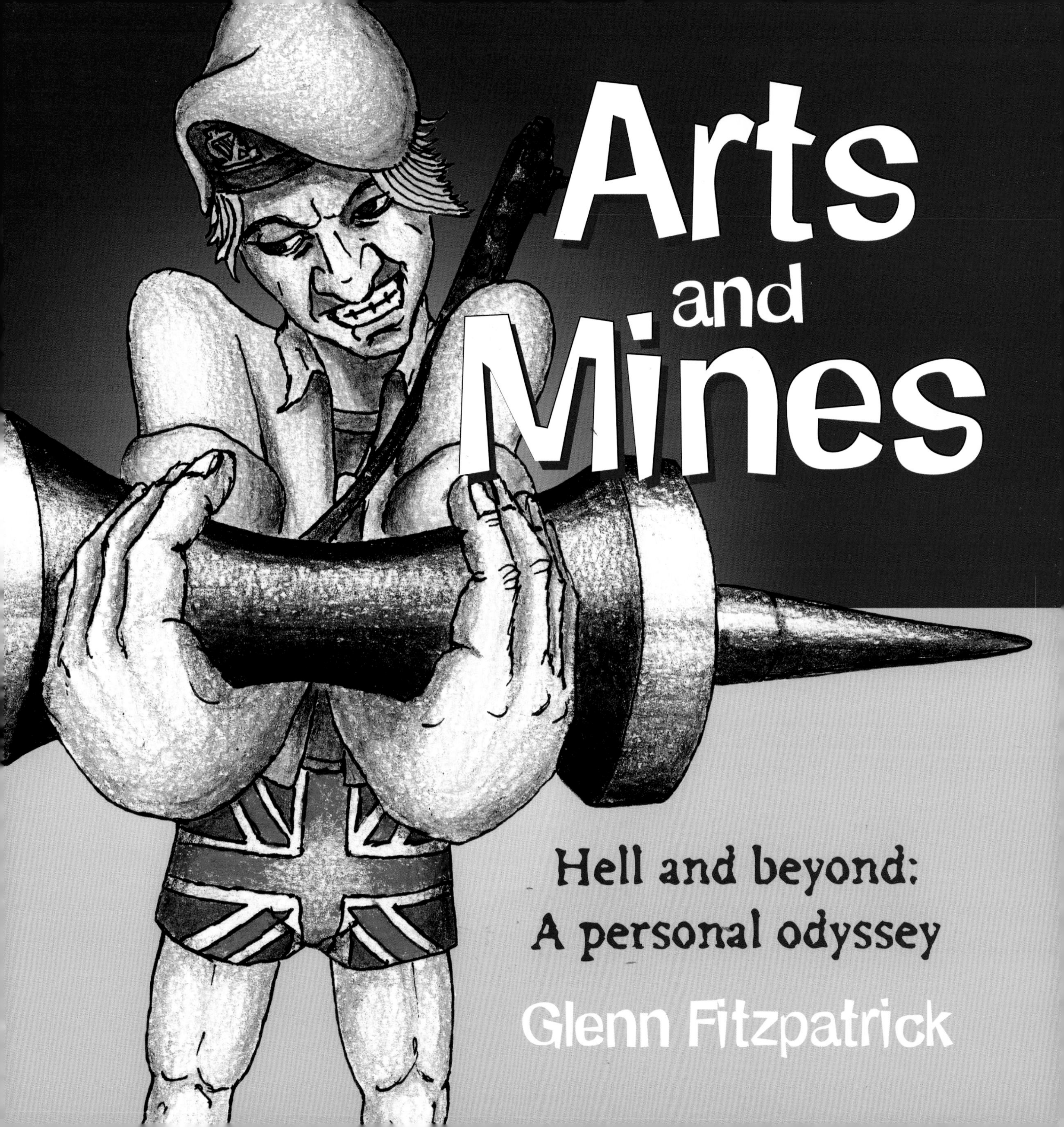
Arts
and
Mines
Hell and beyond:
A personal odyssey
Glenn Fitzpatrick

Published by Aerocomm Ltd
The Gatehouse, 104 Lodge Lane, Grays, Essex, RM16 2UL
United Kingdom
T: +44 (0)1375 427014
F: +44 (0)1375 404478
www.aerocomm.aero

Printed in the UK

ISBN 978-0-9554195-6-0

Dedicated to the memory of great friends and family
who passed on way before their time:

Jonathon Kelly (the Rooster)
Matthew Chadwick (Chuggy)
Andrew Byrne
Jason Morgan
Billy Outram
Derek Fitzpatrick
Magilla Fitzpatrick

Lads, I'm just glad to know that you're
warming up heaven for us.

So, Fitzy – who is he?

Gravesend, 1971. A tough town with attitude. Disposable workers with no real prospects but unbreakable spirit. Into this sub-working class environment, Fitzy (aka Glenn Fitzpatrick) was born. Or maybe erupted – depends who's talking. A bit of a wild child in a good Irish Catholic family; he didn't mind getting into bother or trouble, but he always avoided sin. Fine line there. Hmm.

Hanging out, the Lion Garage, no fear of weirdos – *au contraire.* Fitzy and friends found sport in weirdo baiting and kept fit by running away. But the place kind of policed itself and pervy oddballs didn't last long in the realm.

His dad was a scaffolder, British Army veteran, old-fashioned disciplinarian. It was a thick ear for Fitzy and his brothers and sisters if they were lippy but that did no harm in the manners department. John Fitzpatrick came home after a hard day's work telling his son don't do what I do, get a life, so like a teenage know-it-all Fitzy left school and almost followed in his footsteps, just about but not quite. His mother Linda kept asking what will you do? Hairdressing he said because it looked easy. Linda was shocked, John said son, I will always love and support you no matter what – are you gay? (He's SO not.) But it was a short-lived career. Fitzy found it impossible to make some right horrible women look nice, knowing it would be a waste of a good shovel.

And drugs, ah drugs. Everyone smoked blow (cannabis), so naturally Fitzy did too. At 15, he was a full-time stoner. The mellow life created a lazy, stoned armchair society with no flamboyant role models. Fitzy woke up one day thinking there had to be more to life. If anyone or anything was going to sort him out, it would be the Army. So he signed up.

On 28 January 1990, he began basic military training and excelled. Training was hard; Fitzy loved it. Top days. He joined the Queens Royal Irish Hussars in August and shipped off to Germany. Just two months later, the regiment headed for the Middle East to help liberate Kuwait. First came months in the desert training, discovering amusing things, then the shock of the Gulf War. 100 hours in battle, too much, too young. Fitzy went home changed for life by experiences he did not know how to express or comprehend.

He left the Army in 1993, still confused and lost, and found it difficult fitting into society. The dole was bad; the job situation worse. Drugs helped forget and put the war experience behind him, but relief was temporary. He found no remedy in this, been there got the t-shirt syndrome. Life was about going forward not back, thought Fitzy. As art was the only thing he had ever been good at, he opted for education in art – a new beginning.

1995. Fitzy started college, heard praise for the first time in education and got the study bug. He enrolled in Kent Institute of Art and Design in 1997. It was a most valuable and positive experience in the decommissioning and restructuring of Fitzy's transition from soldier to artist.

In 1998, Fitzy developed head pains which an MRI scan revealed to be a life-threatening cyst on the carotid artery under the base of his brain. 14 January 1999: the cyst was removed in a nine and a half hour procedure and his life changed forever. This experience also opened a bigger picture to Fitzy, that life is short. He woke up more alive then ever, with a new determination to draw, working to the best of his ability. Without realising it, he began to document his kaleidoscope of experiences.

2000. Fitzy graduated with a 2.1 alongside everyone he had started the course with. He wasn't going to let the operation get in his way.

Not bad for a Gravesend dyslexic war dog said Fitzy. Double not bad when he put on cap and gown again in 2001 to receive his MA in Fine Art.

Newly confident, educated – and lost after leaving another institution. It was hard to be normal, easy to numb the pain with drink. Finally Fitzy found Combat Stress, an organisation that specialises in the rehabilitation of veterans. Help when and where it is needed most.

Fitzy was luckier than some, able to immerse himself in art. It's an outlet and a channel for his energies. Plus – importantly – a way to tell others what it was like to be a hoodie, a junkie, a soldier. The camaraderie, the harsh realities, the struggles. Art may not be the answer to life but it can sure as hell improve it says Fitzy.

So hold this book carefully friend. It may explode in your face with raw emotion. You may be able to smell the blood sweat and tears that went into it, feel the beat of the artist's heart running down its spine, vibrant, alive. You get only one life. This is Fitzy's.

(The overspills and continuation of Fitzy's art journey can be seen on his website www.fitzy593.co.uk Symbols of Society.)

Is time really a healer? Our Government seems to think so. I have sometimes wondered if my problems in the past had anything to do with the handling of depleted uranium rounds. I would love to put my problems behind me but I find it hard to ignore pain. Who can blame me for wondering where my anxiety began?

I don't want to be a bitter person and don't intend to be. All I am saying is exposure to the chemical weapons that we handled does somewhat raise the questions of ethics. I don't believe that anyone in power at the time would have meant us to become ill due to neglect and improper research. These things happen when everyone gets excited and are not actually there themselves. Anyway, all this happened a long time ago so this is no longer a relevant subject.

People make mistakes all the time. Our leader back then in 2005 admitted to getting it wrong when they couldn't find weapons of mass destruction, but he was able to put it behind him and get on with his job.

All I can ever wish for is that our leaders would acknowledge what has gone on and accept the truth of our history. From this they may learn. Then perhaps in time we can all move on...

RADIUM BLAH BLAH
LOOKSFINE
Must be safe to handle if they say it is
It could have done with a bit more testing
Not a word
of mass destruction, but he was
able to put it behind him and get on
with his Job.
All I can ever wish for is that our
would acknowledge what has gone on
accept the truth of our history, from

SO WHERE DOES THIS STORY ACTUALL
START? IT GOES WAY BACK TO MY CHIL
HOOD IN GRAVESEND, TO HAMPTO
CRESCENT AND THE NEIGHBOURHOO
WHERE I GREW UP, HAD MY FIRST SMOK
MY FIRST DRINK, MY FIRST SEX, MY FIRS
EVERYTHING, OR SO IT SEEMS. I WONDE
NOW IF I'VE BECOME THE PERSON I A
BECAUSE OF THAT ENVIRONMENT OR I
SPITE OF IT. SO MANY QUESTIONS. S
WHERE DOES THIS STORY ACTUALL
START? IT GOES WAY BACK TO MY CHIL
HOOD IN GRAVESEND, TO HAMPTO
CRESCENT AND THE NEIGHBOURHOO
WHERE I GREW UP, HAD MY FIRST SMOK
MY FIRST DRINK, MY FIRST SEX, MY FIRS

SO WHERE DOES THIS STORY ACTUALL
START? IT GOES WAY BACK TO MY CHIL
HOOD IN GRAVESEND, TO HAMPTO
CRESCENT AND THE NEIGHBOURHOO
WHERE I GREW UP, HAD MY FIRST SMOK
MY FIRST DRINK, MY FIRST SEX, MY FIRS
EVERYTHING, OR SO IT SEEMS. I WONDE
NOW IF I'VE BECOME THE PERSON I A
BECAUSE OF THAT ENVIRONMENT OR I
SPITE OF IT. SO MANY QUESTIONS. S
WHERE DOES THIS STORY ACTUALL
START? IT GOES WAY BACK TO MY CHIL
HOOD IN GRAVESEND, TO HAMPTO
CRESCENT AND THE NEIGHBOURHOO
WHERE I GREW UP, HAD MY FIRST SMOK
MY FIRST DRINK, MY FIRST SEX, MY FIRS

Growing up in my area (Gravesend, Hampton Crescent) helped you to develop a quasi-sixth sense. You needed this ability for when you were walking home, knowing you might get attacked by a gang known as the Pack.

The Pack was a gang of dogs. They all had owners but these dogs were unattended at night time and were left free to group up and roam the streets looking for people walking home alone to attack. They were notorious and had bitten nearly everyone who lived in their territory, including me.

One time I escaped by climbing up a lamp post and had to wait nearly two hours before the Pack went somewhere else.

These were very sneaky and cunning dogs. They could hide behind cars waiting for a victim to attack. These mutts were like the SAS, signalling and giving each other the nod when ready to attack. It was good training for me and would prove to be quite useful when I was in military training.

I am led to believe that we are on the second generation of the Pack and nothing has changed. Their legacy lives on – beware!

g up in my area (Gravesend, Hampton Crescent) helps one to develop a quasi-s
for when you were in this area walking home alone, knowing you might g
pack. The Pack was a gang of dogs, they all had owners but these dogs w
were left free to group up and roam the streets looking for people w

One time I turned up ... before the 'Pack' went

The Pack

REX
Breed Unknown?
The most plagued minging dog I have ever seen. One bite and you're sure to get aids, not even fleas would go near this thing.

BANDIT
Breed Staf
Frisky Hard nut that thinks he is better at sex than attacking: even more frightening!

JACK
Breed Jack Russ
Suspected ring leader of the pack. A ginger hard bastard with scottish nature. No matter how much you kick him he will never give up the game!

SHEEBA
Breed. German Shepherd.
Big dog Very sneaky, don't let the size deceive you. This mutt is stealth I know because this git Snuck up and bit me!

BLACKFING
Breed More an experiment.
The scout and victim finder. Gives all the signals for their attack. Also the brains!

waited two hours before the Pack went somewhere else.

ogs were notorious and had bitten nearly everyone that lived in their
ere very sneaky and cunning dogs, they would hide behind cars waiting for a v
were like the S.A.S, signaling and giving each other the nod when ready to att
g for me and would prove to be quite useful when I was in military train
e are on the second generation of the pack and nothing has changed. Their

RECREATION

If you did not want to be a part of the trouble making society in our area, there was very much for 16 year olds to do. Getting stoned was our only solution, we would become so letha and mashed that we could not even spell trouble (probably couldn't spell it when we were straight) Getting stoned was normal recreation in our area literally everyone we knew was doing it. was so available it was like it was on tap, it seemed like there were no straight people around, or real role models, so really we did not know any better.

I guess this was the start of the slippery slope but what a session it was getting t The only thing we were interested in was where we could get the best ever smoke from, th was where the quest began, it was like the search for the holy grail!

If you did not want to be a part of the trouble-making society in our area, there was not very much for 16 year olds to do. Getting stoned was our only solution. We would become so lethargic and mashed that we could not even spell trouble (probably couldn't spell it when we were straight).

Getting stoned was normal recreation in our area. Literally everyone we knew was doing it. Dope was so available it was like it was on tap. It seemed there were no straight people around, or real role models, so really we did not know any better.

I guess this was the start of the slippery slope but what a session it was getting there. The only thing we were interested in was where we could get the best-ever smoke. This was where the quest began. It was like the search for the holy grail!

LSD (acid) is not the way forward, especially when you are a young delusional teenager – as if the delinquent mind is not messed up enough as it is.

So here we are tripping out with altered states of mind, everyone's perception being controlled by the mood of the room at the time. Unfortunately for us our mood was plummeting due to two friends, Lee and Tatty, arguing.

They were having a bad trip and arguing over random things. The argument turned into a nightmare when it escalated to the point of Tatty picking up a knife and threatening Lee with it. Even worse, Lee called Tatty's bluff by opening his body up to him and saying, "Come on then, you haven't got the nerve. Do it, do it!"

Tatty without hesitation lunged forward, ramming the knife in toward Lee like he was going for the kill. Lee was very lucky because the hard-ramming knife hit his belt buckle and snapped on impact.

Talk about a chance in a million. Thank God – otherwise we could have had a death on our hands. It freaked us all out. We broke up the fight and threw Tatty out. No one could believe what had happened. It really made me think about taking drugs again!

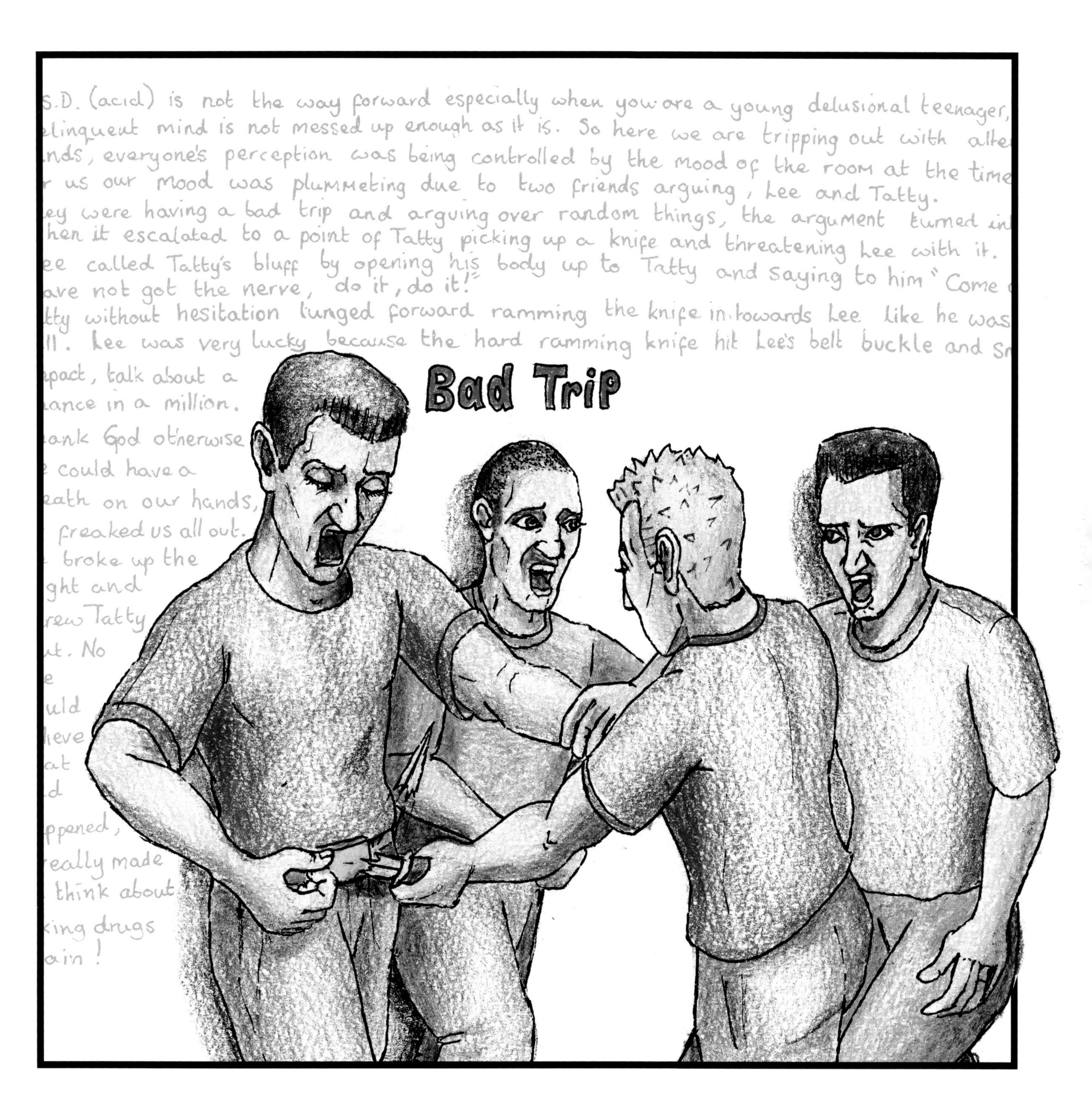

S.D. (acid) is not the way forward especially when you are a young delusional teenager,
elinquent mind is not messed up enough as it is. So here we are tripping out with alte
nds, everyone's perception was being controlled by the mood of the room at the time
r us our mood was plummeting due to two friends arguing, Lee and Tatty.
ey were having a bad trip and arguing over random things, the argument turned in
hen it escalated to a point of Tatty picking up a knife and threatening Lee with it.
ee called Tatty's bluff by opening his body up to Tatty and saying to him "Come
ave not got the nerve, do it, do it!"
tty without hesitation lunged forward ramming the knife in towards Lee like he was
ll. Lee was very lucky because the hard ramming knife hit Lee's belt buckle and sn
Bad Trip
pact, talk about a
ance in a million.
ank God otherwise
e could have a
eath on our hands,
freaked us all out.
broke up the
ght and
rew Tatty
t. No
e
uld
ieve
at
d
ppened,
eally made
think about
king drugs
ain!

Shaft

How is it that whenever I get a job I always seem to get the worse one out of the lot?

My friend (Wiggy) and I were like magnets to a crap job.

One day we were sent to remove the rubble and clean up a newly built lift shaft.

That was o.k. until we discover it was one shaft in particular yes it was the one that nearly every builder pissed (or shit) in, it was disgusting!

This job was evi as soon as you lifted the muddy rubble it was like the earth farted at you. The sme of fart and amm stank that bad it actually made us laugh.

It took us hours remove all the rub but shovel by shove was taking its to and as the ground opened more it released more fa at us. It was the Job from hell, I wa Only to glad to g Out of there and breathe fresh air again.

I really believe the hair up my nostrils perished that day, it real was an experience!

How is it that whenever I get a job, I always seem to get the worst one of the lot**?**

My friend Wiggy and I were like magnets to a crap job. One day we were sent to remove the rubble in a newly built lift shaft and clean it up. That was okay until we discovered it was one shaft in particular. Yes, it was the one that nearly every builder pissed or shit in. It was disgusting.

This job was evil: as soon as you lifted the muddy rubble it was like the earth farted at you. The smell of fart and ammonia stank that bad it actually made us laugh.

It took us hours to remove all the rubbish. Shovel by shovel, it was taking its toll. The more the ground opened, the more fart it released at us. It was the job from hell. I was glad to get out of there and breathe fresh air again.

I really believe the hair up my nostrils perished that day. It was an experience!

The time had come for the newly built incinerator to become active. Its turbines needed to be powered. Its fuel excremental allowed this to become a self-sufficient plant, supplying power to the local areas. Sounds cool but this never reduced anyone's bill.

Nobody was aware of the presence of the Eco lorries (transportation of raw sewage) until they opened their back doors and tipped a load of fresh steamy shit into the conveyors. The only way I can describe the smell is to say it is like being punched up the nasal passage by 100,000 turds! The stench literally ripped its way through the building, penetrating every worker's air space. Everybody was gagging and in that instant they ran out of the building, gasping for fresh air.

My boss came over wondering why I was outside puking. "Stop dossing," he said, "it can't be that bad." I told him if he lasted longer than two minutes in the building, I would work two hours overtime for nothing. He took the challenge and walked inside the plant. He didn't even last a minute. He burst back out and through his gagging managed to say, "Okay, you just go and clean the tea hut for the rest of the day."

The time had come for the newly built incinerator to become active, its turbines needed to be powered. Its fuel excremental allowing this to become a self Sufficient plant therefore supplying power to the local areas. Sounds cool but this never reduced anyone bills.
Nobody was aware of the Eco lorries (Tra
raw sewage) presence until they opened the
and tipped aload of fresh steamy shit onto
The only way I could describe the smell is to
being punched up the nasal passage by 100,0
The stench literally ripped its way t
building penetrating every worker's air
Everybody was gagging and in that in
run out of the building gasping for
My boss came over wondering why I
puking, cheekily he said "Stop dossing, it car
I told him if he lasted longer than t
the building I would work two h
for nothing. He took the cha
walked inside plant, he
last a minute. He came b
out and in a gagging
ECO
ECO
AIR
You dossing? come on get on with it!
× 100,000 = Stench

John's curiosity got the better of him. "What are you doing, walking about with that outboard motor, Glenn?" he asked me.

"I'm waiting for the lads to come back. They're just off nicking a boat. They should be back shortly."

John gave me that 'you're bullshitting' look. "Oh really?" he replied.

"Yeah really – and that's them driving past us right now!" Not even I could believe what I was seeing. How on earth did the lads accomplish that one? There it was, a big boat turned upside down and slapped on top of the van. What a sight! My only explanation for them not being pulled over is that the lads must have had stealth technology in the van.

The inspiration to nick a boat – totally influenced by drink and getting stoned – was the result of talking about how nice it would be to cruise the Medway waters. None of us ever had any money so our solution for achieving our ambition was to get a boat by nicking it.

By nicking a boat, I thought they meant untying a moored boat and just simply sailing it away. What they actually meant was stealing an outboard motor and then lifting a boat out of the water and transporting it from one town to another.

INVISIBLE

"What are you doing walking about with that outboard motor Glenn?" John said curiously looking at me.

"I'm waiting for the lads to come back, there just off nicking a boat, they should be back shortly!"

John gave me that you're bullshitting look and then replied "Oh really".

Yeah really, and that's them driving passed us right now!". Not even I could not believe what I was seeing. How on earth did the lads accomplish that one, there it was, a big boat turned upside down and slapped On top of the van. My only answer for them not being pulled over in a sight like that is the lads must of had stealth technology in the van.

This inspiration towards nicking a boat was totally influenced by drink and getting stoned, and talking about how nice it would be to cruise the Medway waters. None of us ever had any money so our Solution for achieving our ambition was to get a boat, by nicking it. By nicking a boat I really thought they meant untie a moored boat and just Simply sail it away. What it actually meant, stealing an outboard motor and then completely nicking a boat out of the water and transporting it from one town to another

SCARPER

we are in our hot boat out in the Medway waters with all aboard and all systems ready to go.
tarted the outboard motor and off we went for great adventures. It was a lovely day
e sights were fantastic, life couldn't get any better, couldn't get anybetter was right because it was
get worse. We had only travelled down stream for five minutes before we ran out of petrol (Nobody had
d for that one). Basically we were stuck in the middle of the river without a paddle, literally!
matters even worse the police were at the riverside with a tannoy, they said to us "Could the
n the red boat please go to the side, you're holding up the regatta!"

thing we wanted to
go to the side that the
as on, so we
to hand paddle
pposite direction.
that was going on
t persisting on
the outboard motor
as very much a
venture. Rob
up with Mark's
and decided
round to Mark and tell
give it up! As Rob turned
ranked the motor and accid
Rob in the face. (the last pers
orld who you would want to do
because he has the temper of a
bull). Rob went ballistic, and then
chase Mark around the boat, not t
as much room for that. It took a few
to calm Rob down before we could persuad
tart hand paddling with us. Eventually we
to the other side of the river, as soon as our
dry land we were off on our toe's leaving
Our boating days were very short lived!

So there we were in our hot boat out in the Medway waters with all aboard and all systems ready to go. Mark started the outboard and off we went for great adventures. It was a lovely day and the sights were fantastic, life couldn't get any better: couldn't get any better was right because it was about to get worse.

We had only travelled downstream for five minutes before we ran out of petrol (nobody had accounted for that one). Basically we were stuck in the middle of the river without a paddle, literally!

To make matters worse, the police were at the riverside with a tannoy. They said to us, "Could the people in the red boat please go to the side, you're holding up the regatta!" The last thing we wanted to do was go to the side that the police were on, so we started to hand paddle in the opposite direction.

While all that was going on, Mark persisted on cranking the outboard motor, which was very much a pointless exercise. Rob got fed up with Mark's efforts and decided to turn round to Mark and tell him to give it up. As Rob turned, Mark cranked the motor and accidentally elbowed Rob in the face. Rob was the last person in the world who you would want to do that to because he had the temper of a raging bull. Rob went ballistic and then started to chase Mark around the boat – not that there was much room for that.

It took a few minutes to calm Rob down before we could persuade him to start hand-paddling with us. Eventually we made it to the other side of the river. As soon as our feet hit dry land, we were off on our toes, leaving everything behind. Our boating days were very short-lived!

The Army – a new beginning

One day I woke up

It dawned on me suddenly that my gradual decline via drink,

drugs and crime was the most dead of dead-end streets

I really believed that if anything could bring discipline into my life

it would be the Army

I really needed structure and saving from myself, a fresh start...

convinced I got punishe
irby because this lunatic from liverpool found it easier to pronounce my na
& spell Fitzy but he could definitely scousely shout it. Something about my pe
ace, really bugged this instructor so much that he must of found it necessary to
ular basis. Being jailed is every
nightmare, everyone tries to avoid i
ying to this corporal that I
F.c. didn't help my case.
ience in itself, basically
from hell, it is death
place of suffering
this is run by Satan's
, the Provo
an with no
ever. Jail
r half an hour
ith the Provo
ister
elling
ime going to Jail the
personally marched me
room. As soon as we
rporal called out the
t, I was introduced
virgin. The next words
dont bother doing
rs, he's Southern
reak him in!" Said the
and then he went.
alone with the scary provo sergeant. "So...
provo said whilst scowling at me.
Stanley
15 kilo
LBs
I said yes and he s
"I never gave you per
to speak!" Next
pointed towards the
bumper (broom stick
lead weight attach
Stanley, the only fri
will have in this ja
adopt the crucifix
and extend your ar
holding out Stanley!
As I held Stanley ou
really feel my arms
the provo pointed hi
at me and kept say
This torture lasted
an hour, it really kill
thanks alot corpora
Anyway at least I
meet Stanley who pr
be alot more intelli
and interesting than
person who kept
me.

Training in the Army has always been tough, and it can get even harder when you come across a Scouse southerner-hating corporal who can't stand the sight of you.

There were only two southerners in my squadron, Kirby and me. I am convinced I got punished more than Kirby because this lunatic from Liverpool found it easier to pronounce my name. He probably couldn't spell Fitzy but he could definitely scousely shout it. Something about my persona, no doubt my face, really bugged this instructor so much that he must have found it necessary to jail me on a regular basis.

Being jailed is every recruit's nightmare. Everyone tries to avoid it at all costs. Even saying to this corporal that I support Liverpool FC didn't help my case.

Jail is an experience in itself. Basically it is the place from hell. It is death by exercise, a place of suffering and pain. All this is run by Satan's right-hand man, the Provo Sergeant, a man with no mercy whatsoever. Jail usually lasts for half an hour to an hour with the Provo who will administer the most weird and gruelling exercise ever.

For my first time going to jail, the Scouse lunatic personally marched me to the guard room. As soon as we arrived, the corporal called out the Provo Sergeant. I was introduced to him as a jail virgin. "Don't bother doing Fitzy any favours. He's southern scum so just break him in!" said the crazed corporal and then he went.

Now I was left alone with the scary Provo Sergeant. "So... you're Fitzy," the Provo said while scowling at me. I said "Yes" and he screamed "I never gave you permission to speak!"

He pointed toward the floor bumper (a broomstick with a lead weight attached). "That's Stanley, the only friend you have in this jail. Now adopt the crucifix position and extend your arms while holding out Stanley!" As I held Stanley out I could really feel my arms trembling. The Provo pointed his stick at me and kept saying, "Up!" This torture lasted for half an hour. It really killed me – thanks a lot, corporal gitto.

Anyway, at least I got to meet Stanley, who proved to be a lot more intelligent and interesting than the person who kept jailing me.

Snoring can be a huge problem, especially when there are seven other people living with you. All you can hear is the sleeper's elongated hocking noise, usually caused by solidifying phlegm in the back of the throat that can't be swallowed because of its lack of moisture.

My friend Mr Zzz was the culprit snorer. We tried everything to cure this situation but nothing ever worked. All was about to change when our roommate, Jock the Cock, introduced shock therapy to the chronic snorer.

The remedy was simple. Jock straddled above Mr Zzz's head and dangled his large cock (nine inch-ish) in Mr Zzz's face. The next manoeuvre was to keep tapping the patient's forehead until he opened his eyes, and there you have it, miracle cure. The sight, a great ugly Jock with his minging old cock in your face was an instant success. We never heard any more snoring after that!

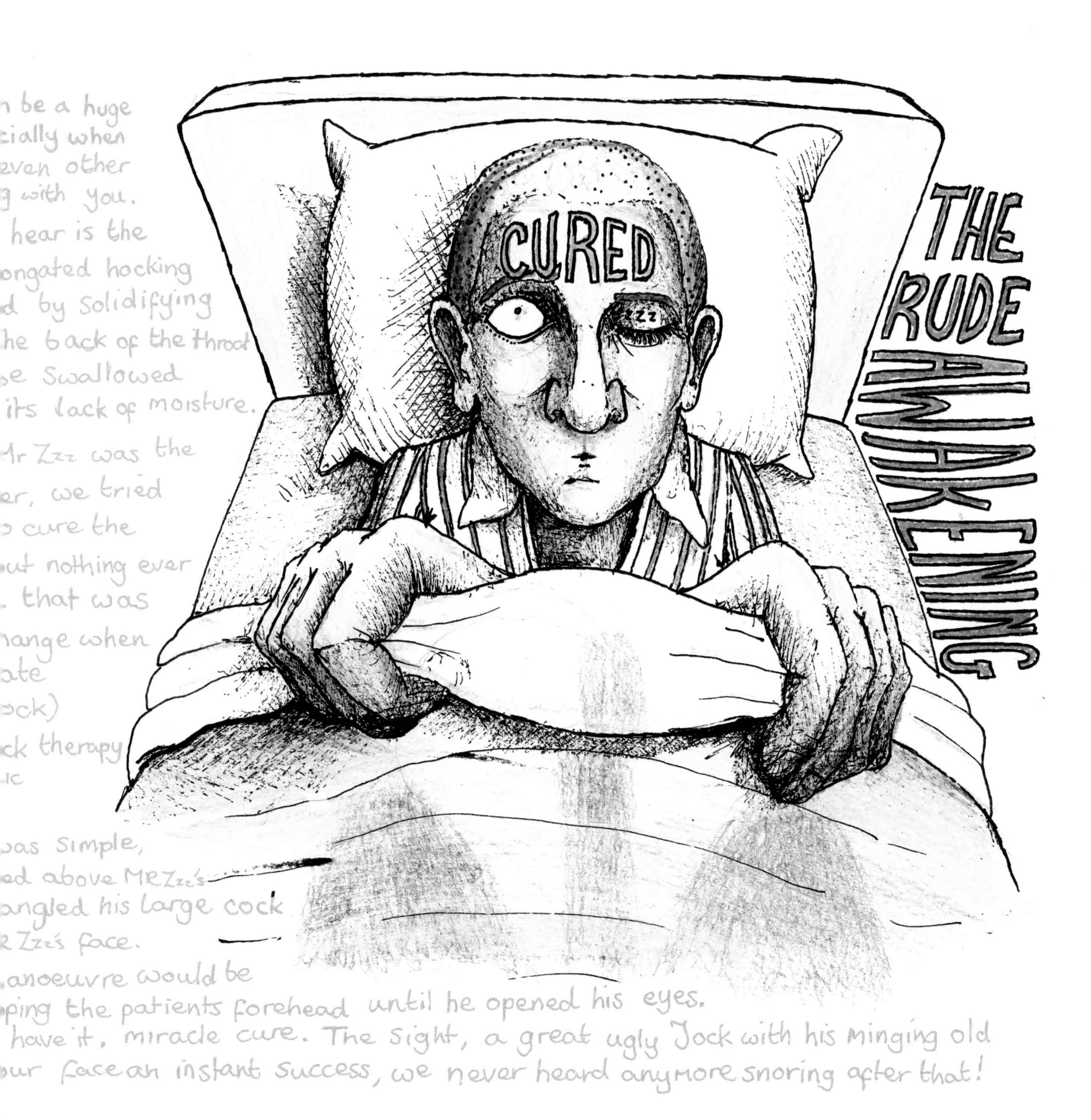
THE RUDE AWAKENING
CURED
Zzz
n be a huge
cially when
even other
g with you.
hear is the
ongated hocking
d by solidifying
he back of the throat
be swallowed
its lack of moisture.
Mr Zzz was the
er, we tried
o cure the
out nothing ever
. that was
nange when
ate
ock)
ck therapy
ic
was simple,
ad above MR Zzz's
angled his large cock
R Zzz's face.
anoeuvre would be
pping the patients forehead until he opened his eyes.
have it, miracle cure. The sight, a great ugly Jock with his minging old
our face an instant success, we never heard anymore snoring after that!

night of escape and evasion and it just happened to be my turn as troop
ader. Our mission was to go on a late night patrol and gather as much i
ssible, prior to that our instructors tipped us off about the route we
ttle did we know but our troop were being
eing stitched up and was heading straight
wards an ambush.

Dirty Tricks

00 AM we all set off on our late night
ssion, it was very dark so vision
s poor even to the point where
u couldn't see your own hand
ving in front of your face.
lowing instruction we headed
ng the tree line towards
destination, all was
ng good and quietly
ced we were ontop
this mission. That was
til we sprung the ambush,
as like the trees come to
, it was our instructors
all I could hear was
of them shouting "find
, he's the troop leader!"
from
where
pounced
patrol,
a sudden
nd myself
quite
y
ed on.
ttacker
ted yanking my

helmet back deliberately
chinstrap would catc
my chin and start chok
here wasn't right, I trie
being captured but my a
to want to stop choking me
when I heard a voice say
I recognised the voice str
was that God forsaken so
that can't stand me and
trying to kill me, I was ru
and options. I started to
got a sudden burst of en
where it was time to figh
way I could get this man o
death was to reach under
and pop the quick release c
worked like a gem. As the
harder at my helmet the
and like a cork flying off
champagne my nemesis we
floor. freeing me up and giving
This must have really annoyed him be
hit the ground he was up again and sw
avoiding his punches I then pounced g
corporal to the ground and then pinned
wanted to land this guy a punch but the
blowing everything I ever trained for stop
was eyeballed him as if to say you will not
picked up my helmet and legged it, ambush free an

A night of escape and evasion and it just happened to be my turn as troop leader. Our mission was to go on a late night patrol and gather as much information as possible. Prior to that, our instructors tipped us off about the route we should take. Little did we know but our troop was being stitched up and was heading straight toward an ambush.

2.00am. We set off on our mission. It was very dark so vision was poor even to the point where you couldn't see your own hand waving in front of your face. Following instructions, we headed along the tree line toward our destination. All was going good and quietly paced. We were on top of this mission. That was until we sprung the ambush.

It was like the trees came to life. It was our instructors and all I could hear was one of them shouting, "Find Fitzy, he's the troop leader!" People from everywhere pounced on our patrol. Someone suddenly grabbed me and I found myself being quite brutally manhandled. My attacker yanked my helmet back deliberately, knowing that the chinstrap would catch at my throat and choke me. Something wasn't right here. I tried to submit to being captured but my attacker didn't seem to want to stop choking me.

The penny dropped when I heard a voice say, "You're mine Fitzy!" I recognised the voice straight away – it was that God-forsaken Scouse corporal and this time he was trying to kill me. I was running out of air and options. I was starting to panic when I got a sudden burst of energy from nowhere. It was time to fight back.

The only way I could get this man off choking me to death was to reach under my chinstrap and pop the quick release catch. That worked a dream. As the corporal pulled harder at my helmet the catch popped and like a cork exploding out of a bottle of champagne, my nemesis went flying to the floor, freeing me up and giving me the air I needed.

This must have really annoyed him because as soon as he hit the ground he was up again and swinging for me. Avoiding his punches, I then pounced, grappling the corporal to the ground and then pinning him. I really wanted to land this guy a punch but the realisation that by doing so I would blow everything I had ever trained for stopped me. All I did was eyeball him to let him know he would not beat me. Then I picked up my helmet and legged it, ambush free and satisfied.

12th July. What a day to join a Northern Irish regiment. This was to be my first impression of what I had gotten myself into, the Queen's Royal Irish Hussars.

Hearing and seeing what goes on was quite a shock to the system. All I could think was, 'Oh no, I'm an English Catholic in an Irish Protestant regiment. Shit.' The people didn't take to new recruits either. Rather than say hello it would be, "Where are you from and what religion are you?" I just knew life wouldn't be too easy after that. I had no choice. In an outnumbered situation like that, all you can do is put on a false smile and adapt!

When I was asked what regiment would I like to join, I replied that I would like to join a London one. I had been told they were recruiting and seeing as I was half Irish, it might be worth considering a London Irish regiment. They couldn't make me sign on the dotted line quick enough...

One thing they could have told me was I was being sent to a nutters' regiment. All I can say is I was very naïve and I was suckered in big time!

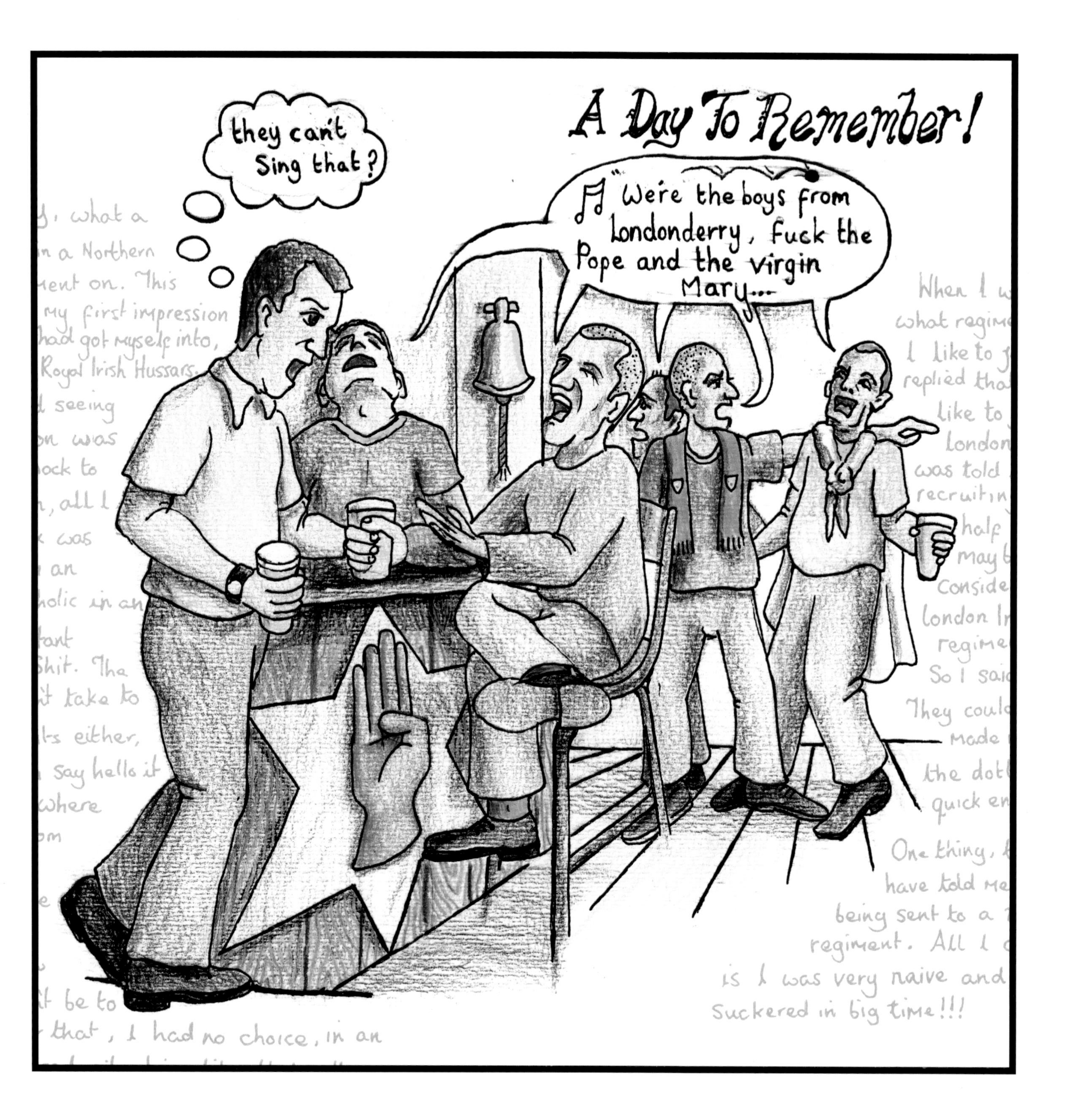
A Day To Remember!
they can't Sing that?
We're the boys from Londonderry, fuck the Pope and the virgin Mary...

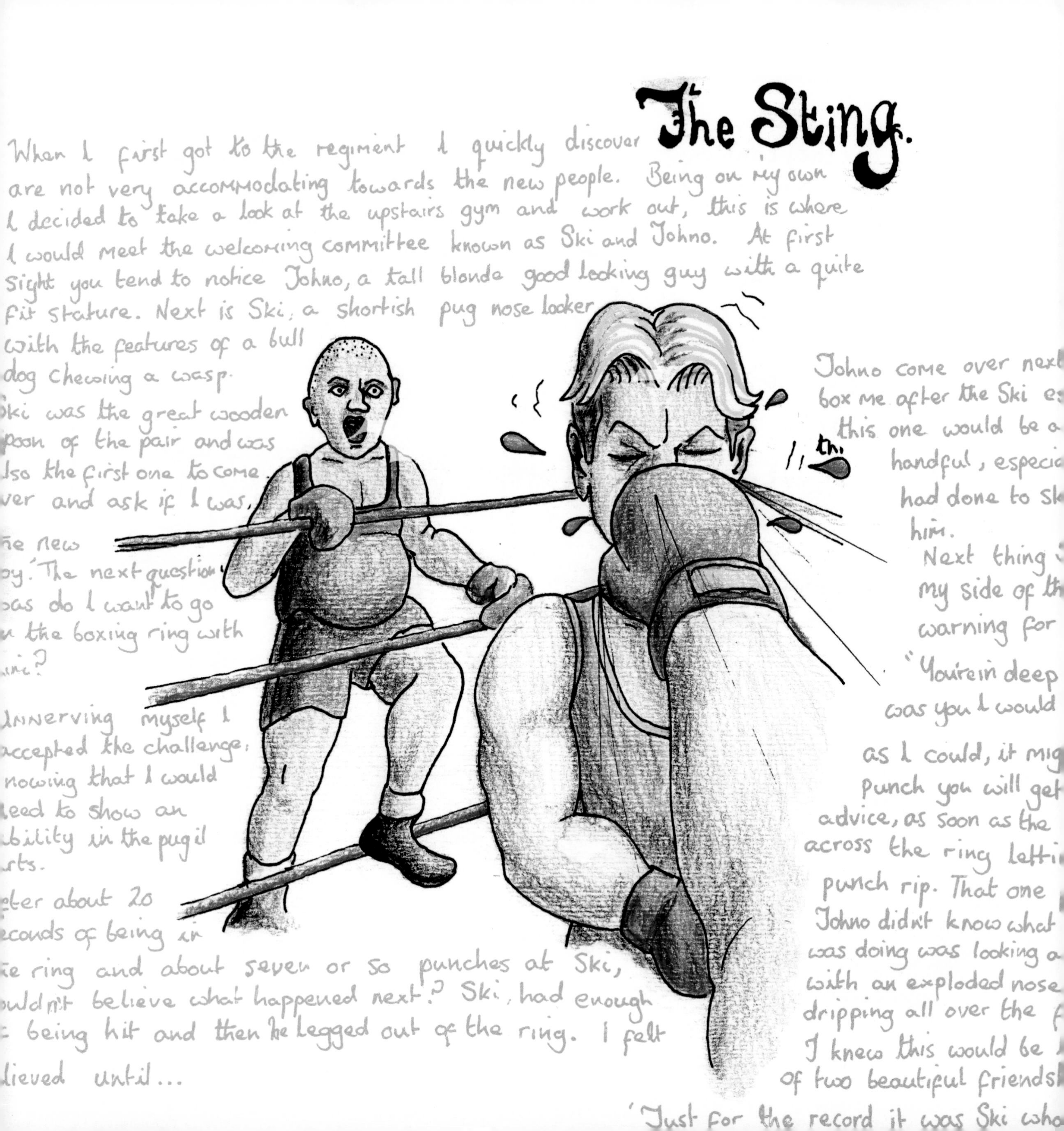
The Sting.
When I first got to the regiment I quickly discover
are not very accommodating towards the new people. Being on my own
I decided to take a look at the upstairs gym and work out, this is where
I would meet the welcoming committee known as Ski and Johno. At first
sight you tend to notice Johno, a tall blonde good looking guy with a quite
fit stature. Next is Ski, a shortish pug nose looker
with the features of a bull
dog chewing a wasp.
ki was the great wooden
poon of the pair and was
lso the first one to come
ver and ask if I was,
ne new
oy. The next question
as do I want to go
n the boxing ring with
Unnerving myself I
accepted the challenge,
nowing that I would
eed to show an
bility in the pugil
rts.
fter about 20
econds of being in
e ring and about seven or so punches at Ski,
uldn't believe what happened next.? Ski, had enough
being hit and then he legged out of the ring. I felt
lieved until...
Johno come over next
box me after the Ski e
this one would be a
handful, especia
had done to Sk
him.
Next thing
my side of th
warning for
"You're in deep
was you I would
as I could, it mig
punch you will get
advice, as soon as the
across the ring letti
punch rip. That one
Johno didn't know what
was doing was looking a
with an exploded nose
dripping all over the
I knew this would be
of two beautiful friends
'Just for the record it was Ski who

When I first got to the regiment I quickly discovered that people are not very accommodating towards newcomers. Being on my own I decided to take a look at the upstairs gym and work out. This is where I would meet the welcoming committee known as Ski and Johno.

At first sight you tend to notice Johno, a tall blond good looking guy and quite fit. Next is Ski, a shortish pug nosed looker with the features of a bulldog chewing a wasp. Ski was the great wooden spoon of the pair and was also the first one to come over and ask if I was "the new boy." The next question was did I want to go in the boxing ring with him?

Unnerving myself, I accepted the challenge, knowing that I would need to show an ability in the pugilistic arts. After about 20 seconds of being in the ring and about seven or so punches at Ski, I couldn't believe what happened next. Ski had had enough of being hit and he legged it out of the ring. I felt relieved until...

Johno came over next, wanting to box me after the Ski escapade. I knew this one would be a bit more of a handful, especially if what I had done to Ski didn't impress him.

Next thing Ski came to my side of the ring with a warning, telling me, "You're in deep shit now. If I was you I would hit him as hard as I could. It might be the only punch you will get." Taking Ski's advice, as soon as the bell rang, I shot across the ring, letting a haymaker punch rip. That one punch said it all. Johno didn't know what had hit him. All he was doing was looking at me in shock with an exploded nose and blood dripping all over the floor. I knew this would be the beginning of two beautiful friendships.

Just for the record, it was Ski who stitched Johno, otherwise I wouldn't have haymakered him.

Everyday life in the Army was certainly different to anything I ever experienced back in the normal world. You always encounter the unexpected.

Nature was calling so I turned to my friend Anto and said, "I'm off to the block for a slash." Anto replied, "Hold on, I'm bursting too, I'll take a walk with ya." So we headed for the toilets.

"Arrgh... finally... that's better, what a relief!" I said to Anto who was standing at the other urinal and snickering. "Ssshhhh, Fitzy listen, can you hear that?" Anto said in a whisper.

As Anto spoke I could hear what he was listening to. It was a strange but speedy knocking noise with a hint of Darth Vader rapidly breathing, and it happened to be coming from the cubicle behind us.

It didn't take a genius to work out what was going on behind this closed door. So I signaled to Anto, 'Let's creep up and take a peek, let this guy know he's been busted.' Anto agreed with a nod. He hand-signing 1... 2... 3... we pounced at the cubical walls and peered over the top, laughing and shouting, "Busted!"

I could not believe what I was witnessing. It was one of our new recruits, Robbo. He was wearing a respirator, had a porno magazine in one hand, cock in the other and was cranking like there was no tomorrow. We could not let this one go, so it was not long before everyone was walking past Robbo doing the Darth Vader noise and breathing the word, "Politician!"

THE POLITICIAN

It was a strange but speedy
knocking noise with a hint of Da
Vader rapidly breathing, and it
happened to be coming from the
cubical behind us.

It does not take a genius to w
out what was going on behind
this closed door. So I
signaled to Anto, let's cre
up, and take a peek. Let t
guy know he has been buste
Anto agreed with a giggling
After hand signaling 1...2...3
we pounced at the cubical
walls and then peered ove
the top laughing and shouti
"Busted!"
I could not believe what I
witnessing, it was one of ou
new recruits Robbo. He w
wearing a respirator, had
porno magazine in one han
Cock in the other and
was cranking away like
there was no tomorrow.
We could not let this
one go, so it was not
before everyone was wal
past Robbo doing the Da
Vader noise breathing th
words "Politician!"

The most frustrating job in the British Army is guard duty. It is an essential part of our military security detail but can be the most dull, mundane, mind-numbing job ever.

Guard duty consists of a 24-hour shift comprising a two-hour stag (shift) on the gate checking ID and cars for any terrorist activity, followed by another two hours on QRF (quick reaction force) entailing a patrol of the perimeter looking for any suspicious movements or unusual packages, a little more interesting than the gate duty but when nothing happens, still incredibly boring.

The third shift, finally, is a two-hour break. This is where the real mental torture begins. On returning to the rest area you can guarantee that someone will be playing porno movies. Good advice: do not ask for it to be turned off. You will only be snarled at and accused of being gay. The torture comes from watching it because you're bored stiff and there is nothing else to do until your next shift. Even worse, you're still in your adolescent phase so being subjected to hours of porn can bring out the worst in your horny inhibitions, leaving you to contemplate the nearest knot hole in the fence.

Sleep is the only other option and that isn't a pretty sight either. On entering the bunk room, you are confronted by a row of wigwams. Lying down and sleeping for a minute, you suddenly need a wee. Finally you get up to go to the toilet. Nightmare. Someone will accuse you of going to the toilet for a sneaky 'throttler'. Just as you fall asleep again, you're woken up for the next stag. It's a night of repetition.

No wonder so many squaddies end up in the red-light district on their night off.

FRUSTRATION

most frustrating Job in the British Army is Guard duty. It is an essential
Military security detail which can sometimes be the most dull mundane mind numbing Job ever. This
ts of a 24hour shift comprizing of a 2 hour Stag (shift) on the gate checking ID and cars for any terrorist
ty, followed by another 2 hours on Q.R.F (quick reaction force) entailing a patrol of the perimeter looking f
spicious movements or
al packages, a little
e interesting than the
uty but when nothing
s is still incredibly
The third shift,
is a 2 hour break,
where the real
torture begins.
urning to the rest
you can always
ntee that someone
e playing porno movies,
dvice, do not ask it be
d off, you will only be snarled
d accused of being gay.
torture being, you're watching
ecause your bored stiff and
e is nothing else to do until your
shift. Even worse your still
ur adolescent phase so being
ected to hours of porn can
out the worst in one's horney
itions, therefore leaving one to
emplate the nearest knot hole in the fence. Sleep is the
other option and that isn't a pretty sight either. Upon
ering the bunk room you are confronted by a row of
-wams. Laying down and sleeping for a minute you suddenly
d a wee, finally you get up to go to the toilet, nightmare,
eone will accuse you of going to the toilet for a sneaky throttler (masturbation).

Just as you fa
asleep again
you're woken u
for the next
Stag, it's a
night of
repetition.

No wonder wh
so many
Squaddies en
up in the red
light district
on their night
off!

GUARD ROOM STASH

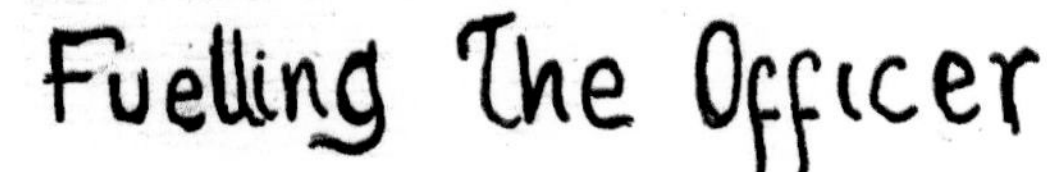
Fuelling The Officer

He insisted I hurry up and then he took over, look at him now!
OC
'MAJOR DIESEL LOVER'
Sometimes being
doesn't pay off,
when you try to
that you're supposed
great care in doing.
The Major and I had alot
do around Canada, problem,
on fuel. I suggested we
one of the tanks.
process of
The Major,
he is, decided to
tube from me
proceeded
like
McDonald's
Bad mistake, he
diesel than I could fill the
Next thing he was coughing and
all I could do at first was laugh and take

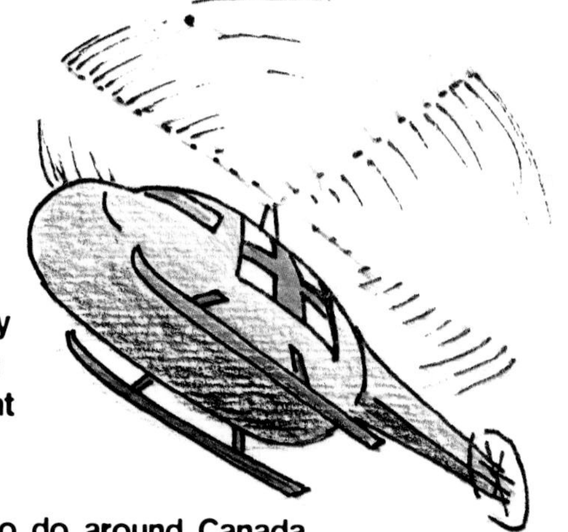

Sometimes being arrogant doesn't pay off, especially when you try to rush a job that you're supposed to take great care in doing.

The Major and I had a lot of driving to do around Canada. Problem: we were low on fuel. I suggested we siphon from one of the tanks. I began the process of siphoning gently. The Major, impatient guy that he was, decided to take the tube from me and then proceeded to suck like you would a McDonald's milk shake.

Bad mistake. He swallowed more diesel than I could fill the Land Rover with. Next thing he was coughing and spluttering, and all I could do at first was laugh and take the piss. That was until he started turning blue. That's when I realised something was wrong. So I called the medic and within minutes the air ambulance arrived. I didn't see the Major for two weeks. After that, he never rushed me anymore... Oh humble pie!

I sometimes wonder if all my misfortunes are related to a simple mistake that I made. At the time, I was the Squadron Leader's driver and I just happened to be out on my own and lost on the prairie of Canada. Like you do, I was praying for a sign. These are pretty much non-existent in this terrain so I kept driving and looking for anything that could give me an indication as to where I was.

After driving for a while, I finally spotted a signpost on the horizon. It was facing away from me so I decided to drive across the strange muddy wasteland to see what the other side could tell me. It read: 'Ancient Indian Burial Ground. Do not cross!'

Why on Earth was this not a double-sided sign? It would have made more sense, I thought while looking at the dirty great track marks that I had made across the site.

I drove off thinking I would probably be cursed for that and hoping that it will be a small curse because it wasn't my fault really.

Any Landmarks
I sometimes wonder if all my misfortunes are related to a simp
that I made. At the time I was the Squadron leader's driver and I just happened to be out
own and lost in the prairie of Canada. Like you do, I was praying for a sign, these are pre
much non existent in this terrain so I kept driving and looking for anything that co
give an indication as to
where I was.
WARNING
Ancient Indian
Burial Ground
Not Cross!
You will be cursed
Pension will be
Ooops
I drove off thinki
I will probably be cu
for that, hopefully
be a small curse
because it wasn't
fault rea
After driving for a while I finally spotted a sign on
the horizon. It was facing back to me so I decided
to drive across the strange muddy waste land
to see what on the other side could tell me.
It read 'Ancient Indian Burial Ground, Do not cross!'
Why on Earth was this not a double sided sign, it
would have made more sense I thought whilst looking
at the dirty great track marks that I made across the ancient burial ground.

Falling Angel, Losing Thy Sole.

e words of wisdom for those who get drunk and have to sleep on the top of a bunk bed, "don't do it!"... For myself it was one of those monumental piss up ts, and believe me it really was that. After saying goodnight to new found friends, I realis would be the beginning of my chores i.e. walk home, find the right block, find bed, climb e top bunk, sleep and try to avoid hangover in the morning.

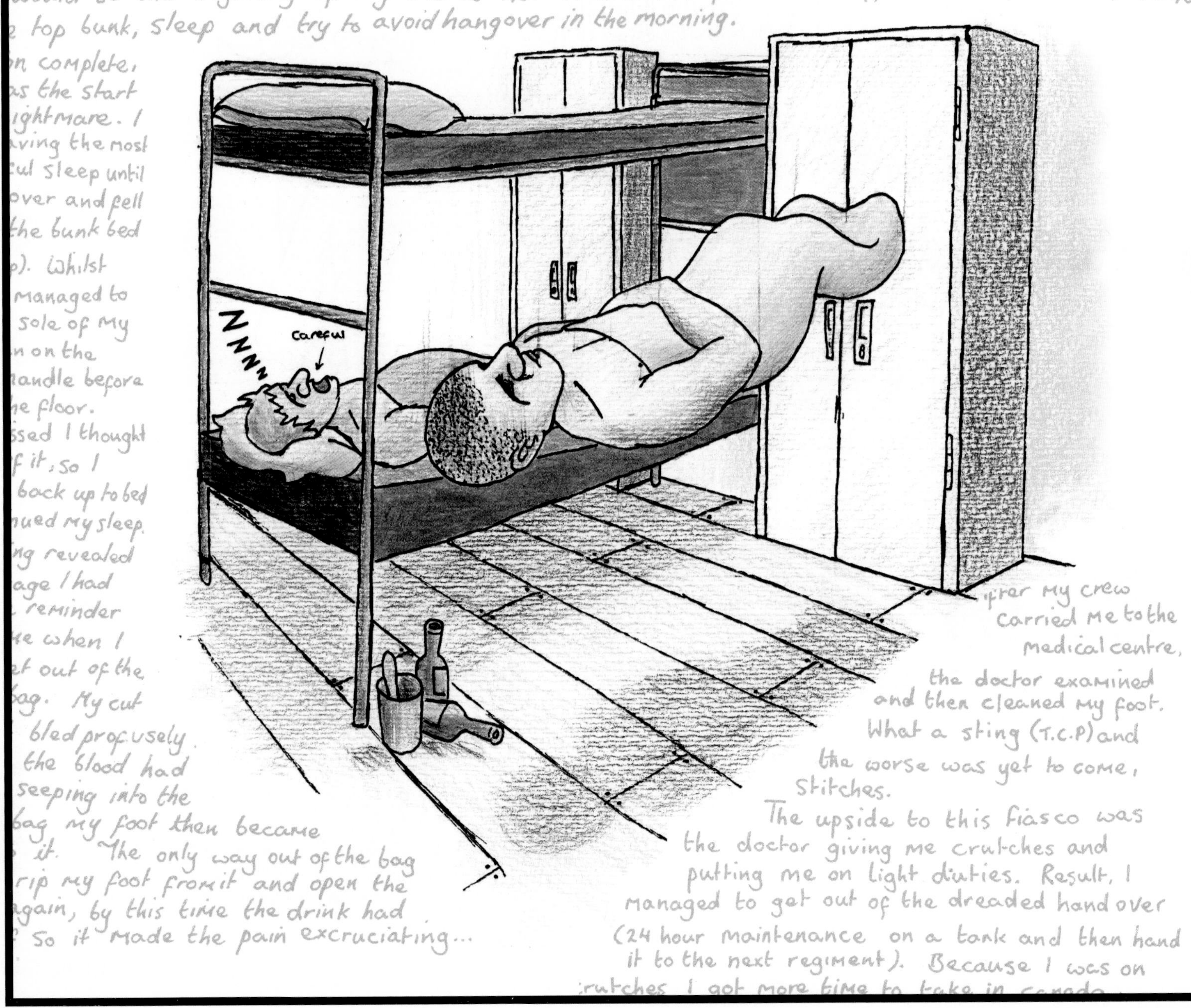

n complete,
as the start
ightmare. I
aving the most
ul sleep until
over and fell
the bunk bed
). Whilst
managed to
sole of my
n on the
handle before
he floor.
ssed I thought
f it, so I
back up to bed
nued my sleep.
ng revealed
age I had
reminder
e when I
et out of the
bag. My cut
bled profusely.
the blood had
seeping into the
bag my foot then became
it. The only way out of the bag
rip my foot from it and open the
again, by this time the drink had
so it made the pain excruciating...
ZZZZ
careful
fter my crew carried me to the medical centre, the doctor examined and then cleaned my foot. What a sting (T.C.P) and the worse was yet to come, Stitches.
The upside to this fiasco was the doctor giving me crutches and putting me on light duties. Result, I managed to get out of the dreaded hand over (24 hour maintenance on a tank and then hand it to the next regiment). Because I was on rutches I got more time to take in canada

Some words of wisdom for those who get drunk and then have to sleep on the top level of a bunk bed: Don't do it! For myself, it was one of those monumental piss-up nghts, and believe me, it really was that. After saying goodnight to new friends, I realised I had quite a task ahead of me, i.e. walk home, find the right block, find bed, climb to the top bunk, sleep and try to avoid hangover in the morning.

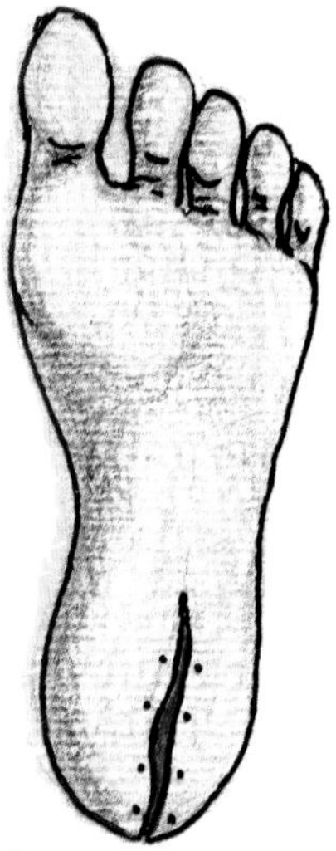

This was the start of a nightmare. I was having the most wonderful sleep until I rolled over and fell out of the bunk bed (six-foot drop). While falling, I managed to cut open the sole of my foot on the locker handle before hitting the floor. Being pissed, I thought nothing of it, so I climbed back up to bed and continued my sleep.

The morning revealed what damage I had done. The reminder came to me when I tried to get out of the sleeping bag. My cut open foot had bled profusely, seeping into the sleeping bag. When the blood dried, my foot then became fused to it. The only way out of the bag was to rip my foot from it and open the wound again. By this time the drink had worn off so the pain was excruciating...

After my crew carried me to the medical centre, the doctor examined and then cleaned my foot. What a sting (TCP) and the worst was yet to come: stitches.

The upside of this fiasco was the doctor giving me crutches and putting me on light duties. Result: I managed to get out of the dreaded handover (24 hour maintenance on a tank and then hand it to the next regiment). Because I was on crutches, I got more time to take in Canada. Good old sympathy sticks.

The Munchies

Getting drunk and stoned is not the greatest Idea in the world, especially when there is no food around and you get the ttack of the munchies. Hunger can nd up putting Oneself on the most xtreme of missions, just to make he mission even more impossible ne needs to be Caned.

he chosen mission between y friend (Stretch) and I as called 'Operation o money no food'. owever don't let aving no money come the object of efeat, a mission ke this needs ball d initiative.

tretch and I took it oon ourselves to go to e vending machines, th hammers, food was i ght.

ter whacking the machine ss about fifteen times and y cracking the glass, we k was time to abort mission legging it!

'Plan B' The rations?

Heading back to base idea of the ration store came to mind. knowin this place was the 'Fort knox' of tin food would an alternative way of getting in. Through the roof.... Bad idea no2.

After climbing out the window onto the roof thre storeys up, I began to rem the roof tiles trying to mak hole I could drop in through keep in mind I was still was at this point, upon removal lost my footing and began to slide towards the edge of the r In a second my life flashed before my eyes, I could see th accident from hell heading my w Fortunately for me Stretch was there for me. Some how he managed to reach out and gr me just before I went over the edge, Nine lives or what? Another mission aborted.

The best idea came right at the last minute... go to bed and wake for breakfast in the morning.

Getting drunk and stoned is not the greatest idea in the world, especially when there is no food around and you get an attack of the munchies. Hunger can drive you to the most extreme of missions. Just to make the mission even more impossible, you need to be caned.

The chosen mission between my friend Stretch and me was called 'Operation No Money No Food'. However, we weren't going to let having no money defeat us. A mission like this needs balls and initiative. Stretch and I took it upon ourselves to have a go at the vending machines with hammers. Food was in sight. But after whacking the machine about fifteen times and only cracking the glass, we knew it was time to abort mission by legging it!

Plan B – The rations?

As we headed back to base, the idea of the ration store came to mind. This place was the Fort Knox of tinned food, so we knew it would take an alternative way of getting in. Through the roof... Bad idea No 2.

After climbing out the window onto the roof three storeys up, I began to remove the roof tiles, trying to make a hole I could drop in through. Keep in mind I was still wasted at this point. As I removed a tile, I lost my footing and began to slide towards the edge of the roof. In a second my life flashed before my eyes, I could see the accident from hell heading my way. Fortunately Stretch was there for me. Somehow he managed to reach out and grab me just before I went over the edge. Nine lives or what?

Another mission aborted. The best idea came right at the last minute... go to bed and wake for breakfast in the morning.

I was out on the town in Germany with my squaddie mates when unfortunately I got lost. I was over fifty miles away from my base, couldn't speak German and was skint. Solution: bunk a taxi.

I managed to blag a taxi and somehow convinced the driver he would be paid as soon as we got back to the barracks. Finally we arrived, I got the driver to park outside another regiment's block (well I didn't want to get my own unit into trouble). I told the driver I was just popping into the block to get his money. Problem: he got out of the car and followed me into the block. I walked straight into the block toilets and he was still right behind me. Time now for evasive action... I locked the door behind me and opened the window. All I could do was jump out and leg it back to my own block.

I made it back and to my surprise I could see into the block next door. There were the Military Police and the taxi driver waking everyone up trying to find me. I knew my block would be next. Time to hide. So I ran up to the gym and hid in a box in the attic until the coast was clear. It worked, result...

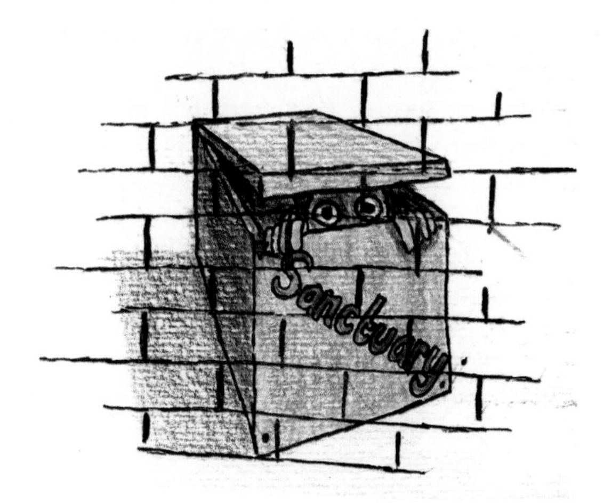

The Great Escape

via the bog.....

n the town in Germany with
mates, unfortunately I got
s over fifty miles away from
ouldn't speak German, and
. Solution, bunk a taxi.

to blaggy a taxi, somehow
the driver he would be paid
s we got back to the barrack
rrived, I got the driver to park
her regiment's block (well I didn't
my own unit into trouble). I told
was just popping into the block
oney, problem, he got out of the
owed me into the block. I walked
the block toilets and he was still
me, time now for evasive action.
a cubical telling him "one moment", I w
nd opened the window beside me. All I could do was
ack and to my surprise I could see into the block next door, there was the Military police and the
ng everyone up trying to find me, I knew my block would be next. Time to hide, so I run up to the
box in the attic until the coast was clear. It worked, result...

Daft, stupid and naïve. That about summed me up, especially when it came down to impressing one woman that I met and really fancied. This German beauty could turn most of us men into putty. Unfortunately Chloe had one flaw: she was a very influential super sexy junkie!

One night my friends and I decided to go out raving with Chloe and had the best time ever. Nobody wanted the night to end so Chloe suggested we take the party back to her place. As soon as we arrived, she got a load of drugs out and said, "Would you and the boys like to do some lines with me?" Because we all fancied getting into Chloe's good books, we all simultaneously responded, "Yes please."

Chloe then proceeded to cut up the drugs, offering them to us one by one. Jokingly, I mentioned to her that the lines were a bit shy (like I had had any bigger). Instantly Chloe replied in an urgent German accent, "No no Glenn, very strong!" Oh well. I thought beggars can't be choosers, so I snorted up what I thought was a puny little line. This little line hit me like a sledge hammer and within minutes of taking it I was full on rushing out of my head and feeling wicked. I turned to my friend and said, "Can you feel this gear, Pete? It's absolutely mental, isn't it?" Pete was so zapped he'd lost the power of speech so I turned to Chloe and said, "Where did you get this speed? It's amazing!" Just as I said that, she cut in and said, "Speed... no, heroin!"

Oh my God: heroin, the only drug that I swore never to take and here I was on it. My buzz went downhill rapidly. I don't remember much after that. All I could hope was the guard at the time would not be able to spot that I was on heroin as I walked back into the barracks. I gave Chloe a wide berth after that.

ft stupid and naive, that about summed me up especially when it came
wn to impressing one woman that I met and really fancied. This German
auty could almost turn most of us men into putty
eortunately Chloe had one flaw, she was a very
luential super sexy junkie!
e night my friends and I decided to go out ra
th Chloe and had the best time ever, nobody
anted the night to end so Chloe suggested we
ke the party back to her place.
soon as we arrived Chloe got
ad of drugs out and then she
to me "would you and the boys
to do some lines with me?"
ause we all fancied getting into
e's good books we all
ultaneously responded
ing " yes please."
e then proceeded
ut up the drugs
ring to us one
ne. Jokingly
entioned to
that the lines
e a bit shy, like
d any bigger...
t instant Chloe
ed in an urgent German
ent "No No Glenn, very strong!"
ell I thought beggars can not be
sers, so I snorted up what I thought was to be a puny little line. This little line hit me like a
ge hammer and with in minutes of taking it I was full on rushing out of my head and feeling wick
n turned to my friend and said " Can you feel this gear Pete, its absolutely mental is'nt it?
was so zapped he lost the power of speach so I turned to Chloe and said "Where did you get this
, it's amazing?" Just as I said that she instantly cut in and said " Speed... no heroin!"
God heroin, the only drug that I swore never to take and here I was on it, my buzz went down hill after tha
remember much after that. All I could hope was the guard at the time would not be able to spo
I was on heroin as I walked back into the barracks. I gave Chloe a wide birth after that
Oops

Please Go Home

as a usual night out on the town with
ads, everyone was fine and dandy. That
until some big mad crazed
an burst into the pub making
presence known. The next thing I
was this guy barging through the
d spilling everyone's drink that
nocked. I don't know why but
guy came straight over to my
let two punches go which
ected both of my mates'
. Then he laughed
walked over to the
side of the
my two
ds were just stood
with their mouths
open and a look
read did that
lly happen?
ing the two
I was with I could
assume they pissed
guy off before,
e shagged his
riend, I would not
it passed them.
guy definitely
oked a reaction
use a load of
d thirsty new recruits were
ning to get him outside, we
not bothered, why should they be?

As the guy was leaving the pub I thought
seen enough of casualties so decided
over and tell him what was going to ha
to him if he did not leave for home qu
This guy made out he did not understand, g
heard him speaking English earlier that n
Anyway so much for favours, this gu
launched into an attack cutting my ch
open and blacking my eye, he was li
mad gorilla. All I could do was c
into a boxing stance and wait for
lunatic to leave his attack wide ope
opportunity came and I seized it, as
swung wide readying his next pu
shot my punch straight through the
of him and broke his Jaw. It pu
stop to this guy within seconds, eve
arms just flopped to the side of h
It was too late for me, I now was ac
and was going for the kill, it was
didn't even know myself. The pu
did not stop until the Militar
broke me up and took me away
was held in their cells awa
questioning, this is where I g
that I hospitalised this gu
busting his nose and breaki
Jaw in two places, I was
never did I think I could do
to someone, this frightened m
I was told if proved guilty I woul
to prison. Lucky for me the c
were dropped on account of self d
I had about ten witnesses claim

It was a usual night out on the town with the lads, everyone was fine and dandy. That was until some big, mad, crazed German burst into the pub making his presence known. The next thing I saw was this guy barging through the crowd, bumping people and spilling everyone's drink. I don't know why but this guy came straight over to my lot, let two punches go which connected with both of my mates' faces. Then he laughed and walked over to the other side of the pub.

My two friends just stood there, still with their mouths wide open and a look that read, 'Did that really happen?' Knowing the two that I was with, I could only assume they'd pissed this guy off before, maybe shagging his girlfriend; I wouldn't put it past them.

This guy definitely provoked a reaction because a load of blood-thirsty new recruits were planning to get him outside. But we weren't bothered, so why should they be? I thought I had seen enough casualties so decided to go over as the guy was leaving the pub and tell him what was going to happen to him if he did not leave for home quickly! He made out he did not understand. Git, I'd heard him speaking English earlier that night.

Anyway, so much for favours. He launched into an attack, cutting my cheek open and blackening my eye. He was like a mad gorilla. All I could do was cover into a boxing stance and wait for this lunatic to leave his attack wide open. The opportunity came and I seized it. As he swung wide, readying his next punch, I shot my punch straight through the centre of him and broke his jaw. It put a stop to this guy within seconds. Even his arms just flopped to the side of him.

It was too late for me. I was now activated and going for the kill. It was like I didn't even know myself. The punishment didn't stop until the Military Police broke it up and took me away. I was held in their cells awaiting questioning. This is where I got told that I'd hospitalised this guy, busting his nose and breaking his jaw in two places. I was shocked. I never thought I could do that to someone. It frightened me. I was told I could go to prison. Luckily for me, the charges were dropped on account of self-defence. I had about ten witnesses claim he attacked me first. These were all good customers!

Brilliant, a weekend off. Destination: England. It's a long drive from Germany but a worthwhile journey. Car: Escort XR3i. Trendy once upon a time. Crew: Darren, Ski and Fitzy (AKA me). The drive to be taken in shifts, Darren for the first one (the only one), me for the next (the late one) and Ski for none (couldn't be trusted, however he makes the greatest co-pilot).

It was my shift and everything was running quite smoothly. That was until some maniac driver started tailing us very closely with full beams on which were glaring into my rear view mirror and nearly blinding me. Trying to be sensible, I slowed down so he could overtake. Unbelievably, he level-pegged our car while flashing his interior light on and off.

This driver was really annoying us so I decided to give him my death stare, hoping that would scare him off. Looking across I was astounded. The man in the other car was massive, a real monster. Even worse, he was naked and viciously masturbating while driving and staring back at us. I had to look back at the road and shake my head in disbelief.

I looked at Ski for confirmation that I was not the only one who could see what was going on. I had to ask him, "Did you see that?" Ski, with a look of horror on his face, replied, "Yeah, and he's still there, fucking wanking at us!"

"Okay Ski, what shall we do? Pull over and do him or what?" Judging by the size of this guy, I think he would have eaten us for breakfast, and a nutter like this might have a gun.

"Put your foot down!" Ski said, the answer I was hoping for. With my foot pressed full on the accelerator and driving absolutely flat out, we could not shake off this brown Volvo-driving wanking lunatic. It wasn't until Ski suddenly pointed to a sign coming up rather rapidly and shouted, "Dunkirk!" With a hard turn on the steering wheel, we screeched into the turning, just missing the sign by inches and, nearly crashing, we finally managed to give the wanker the slip.

In all of this commotion, Darren was thrown around the back seat of the car. Waking up, he shouted, "What the fuck's going on?" We tried to explain what happened. Darren didn't believe us and replied, "Would you two stop bullshitting for a living?"

WANKER 1

nt, a weekend off, dasting from Germany to England,
Journey worthwhile. Car, Escort XR3i trendy once upon a time. Crew, Darren, Ski and Fitzy (AK
rive to be taken in shifts, Darren for the first one (the only one), me for the next (the late one), and
one (couldn't be trusted, however he makes the greatest Co-pilot). It was my Shift and everything
ng quite smoothly, that was until some maniac driver was tailing us very closely with full bear
were glaring into my rear view mirror nearly blinding me. Trying to be sensible I slowed down so
could over-take. unbelievable, the driver level pegged our car whilst flashing his interior light on and
river was really annoying so I decided to give him my death stare, hopefully that would scare him
g across astounded me, the man in the other car was massive, a real monster, Even worse he was n
viciously masturbating whilst driving
g back at us. I had to look back
road and shake my head in
ief.

I look
for confirmation that
Only one who could see what was
I had to ask him "did you see that?
Ski with a look of horror on his face replied
and he's still there fucking wanking at us!"
"Ok Ski what shall shall we do, pull over and do him
Judging by the size of this guy I think he would ha
us for breakfast, and a nutter like this might have a
"Put your foot down!" Ski said the answer I was hoping
With my foot pressed full on the accelerator and driving absolutely
out, we could not shake off this brown Volvo driving wanking luna
It wasn't until he suddenly pointed to a sign coming up rather rapidly
shouts "Dunkirk". With a hard turn on the steering wheel we screeched in
turning just missing the sign by inches and nearly crashing we finally managed
give the wanker the slip. In all of this commotion Darren was thrown around th
Seat of the car. Waking up Darren shouted "what the fuck's going on?". We tried to ex

WAR – IT'S WHAT SOLDIERS TRAIN FOR. IT'S
WHAT THEY DO. THEY LEARN
IT'S AN HONOUR TO FIGHT. THEY WATCH
THE BUILD-UP TO WAR WITH FASCINATION,
FEEL THE BRAVADO IN THE RANKS,
SWALLOW THE IMMEASURABLE EGO DOCTRINE.
THAT'S HOW IT WAS IN THE GULF WAR.
BY THE TIME IT CAME, WE WERE LIKE THE
GREYHOUND READY TO CATCH THE HARE.
THE REALITY WAS QUITE DIFFERENT.
THE BLOOD WE TASTED WAS THE
SAME AS OUR OWN, THE ENEMY WE CHASED
LIKE OUR KIN: THE REALITY, THE SHAME!

There comes a time in your life when a person of rank will try volunteering you to kill yourself by testing if the air surrounding is okay for him to breathe.

I was told to do a sniff test – check if the air was poisonous or not. For once in my life I thought, 'Hang on, why should I be the guinea pig, what makes him so different from me, what gives him the right to order me to my own death?' In that moment, I realised he was only a human the same as me, so I exercised my right as a human and said, "Fuck off... sir, but you can be my guest!"

He harassed me for about five minutes after I told him to do one. In the end, he gave up telling me off and then angrily did the sniff test himself. Unfortunately for me there was no gas in the air. I was expecting this officer's eyes to dilate and go bloodshot with the effect of being poisoned by the air. Nothing happened and all I could see in this man's eyes was rage at me. That's when I knew I would be in the shit.

I did hope that his sniff was going to teach him a lesson but no, he decided to teach me a lesson instead. For my sins, I got extra guard duties and had to clean out the portaloos for a week. Still, I believe it is better to refuse a sniff after a gas attack and get in trouble than to die...

I would gladly die fighting but I refuse to die testing!

This is not an SCUD airfreshener

BE MY GUEST

There comes a time in your life when a person of rank will try
Volunteering you to kill yourself by testing if the air surrounding
is o.k. for him to breathe.
I was told to do a sniff test, check if the air was poisonous or not. For or
in my life I thought hang on, why should I be the guinea pig, what makes him
different from me, what gives him the right to order me to my own death?
In that moment I
realised he was onl
human the same as
So I exercised my rig
as a human and sai
Fuck off ... Sir, but you
can be my guest!"
He harassed me for abo
minutes after I told him
do one, in the end he g
up telling me off and
angrily did the sniff tes
himself. Unfortunately f
me there was no gas in
air. I was expecting this
Officer's eyes to dilate a
go blood shot with the ef
of being poisoned by the
Nothing happened and a
could see in this man's
eyes was rage at m
that's when I knew
would be in the shit
I did hope that his sniff was go
to teach him a lesson but no, he
decided to teach me a lesson instea
For my sins I got extra guard duti
and had to clean out the portaloos
a week. Still I believe it is better to refus
a sniff after a gas attack and get in trouble
rather than die...

"I would gladly die fighting
but I refuse to die testing!"

Yeah right

Fitzy, you can do the sniff test!

Meet your match

“Sir, we are in the middle of a live firing range. Don’t tell me we are not lost!” I said to my replacement commander (Mr C) who was fumbling with his map.

“Oh yes, I see what you mean Fitzy, just give me a second and I will get us out of here,” answered Mr C with a somewhat confused look on his face.

This made me realise how lucky I was when I had Pixie as commander. This new guy was driving me mad, and now we were about to be blown out of existence if we did not do something soon. “Sir, while you’re still looking at the map, may I suggest we high speed reverse out of here for a safer place?” I said.

“Oh yes, very good idea Fitzy. Carry on,” he said like one of the members from ‘Carry On Up the Kyber’.

I knew from the first day of meeting Mr C life was going to be more challenging. This was a very new guy, fresh out of officer training, so he was very keen and eager to prove himself. This made him a bit gung-ho. I did get a bit of the green-eyed monster because he was all of the things I was not. He was (not being gay) handsome, intelligent, athletic and rich – he had to be because he never bought a round. The only thing he did not have was experience. Even worse, he thought he knew it all.

When you meet people like this, you cannot help thinking, ‘Now we are screwed.’ He scared me because here we were, there was a lot of artillery firing over the top of us and we were going to die. I wouldn’t have minded but the war had not even started, so I made the decision to go back the way we came. Eventually we found our unit again and I could not believe it, Mr C thanked me for my patience and for getting us back. This was the beginning of our understanding each other. I still knew that I was going to have my work cut out.

LOST

we are in the middle of a live firing range, dont tell me we are not lost!" I said
ny replacement commander (Mr C) who was fumbling with his map.

es, I see what you mean Fitzy, just give me a second and I will get us out of here."
ered Mr C with a some what confused look on his face.
made me realize how lucky I was when I had Pixie as commander.
new guy was driving me mad, and now we were about to be
out of existence if we did not do something soon.

while you're still looking at the map may I suggest we high
reverse out of here
safer place?" I said.

, Very good Idea Fitzy
on", he said like one of the
ers from Carryon up the khyber.

w from the first day of meeting Mr C life was going to be more challenging. This was a very
guy, fresh out of Officer training, so he was very keen and eager to prove himself, this made hi
gung ho. I did get a bit of the green eyed monster because he was all of the things I was not, he
(Not being gay) handsome, intelligent, athletic and rich, he had to be because he never bought a
d. The only thing he did not have was experience, even worse he thought he knew it all,
you meet people like this you can not help thinking now we are screwed. He scared me
se here we are, there is alot of artillery firing over the top of us and we are going to die,
uldn't mind but the war had not even started, so I made the decision to go back the
we came. Eventually we found our unit again and I could not believe it Mr C thanked me
y patience and for getting us back. This was the beginning of our understanding each other.
I knew that I was going to have alot of work cut out.

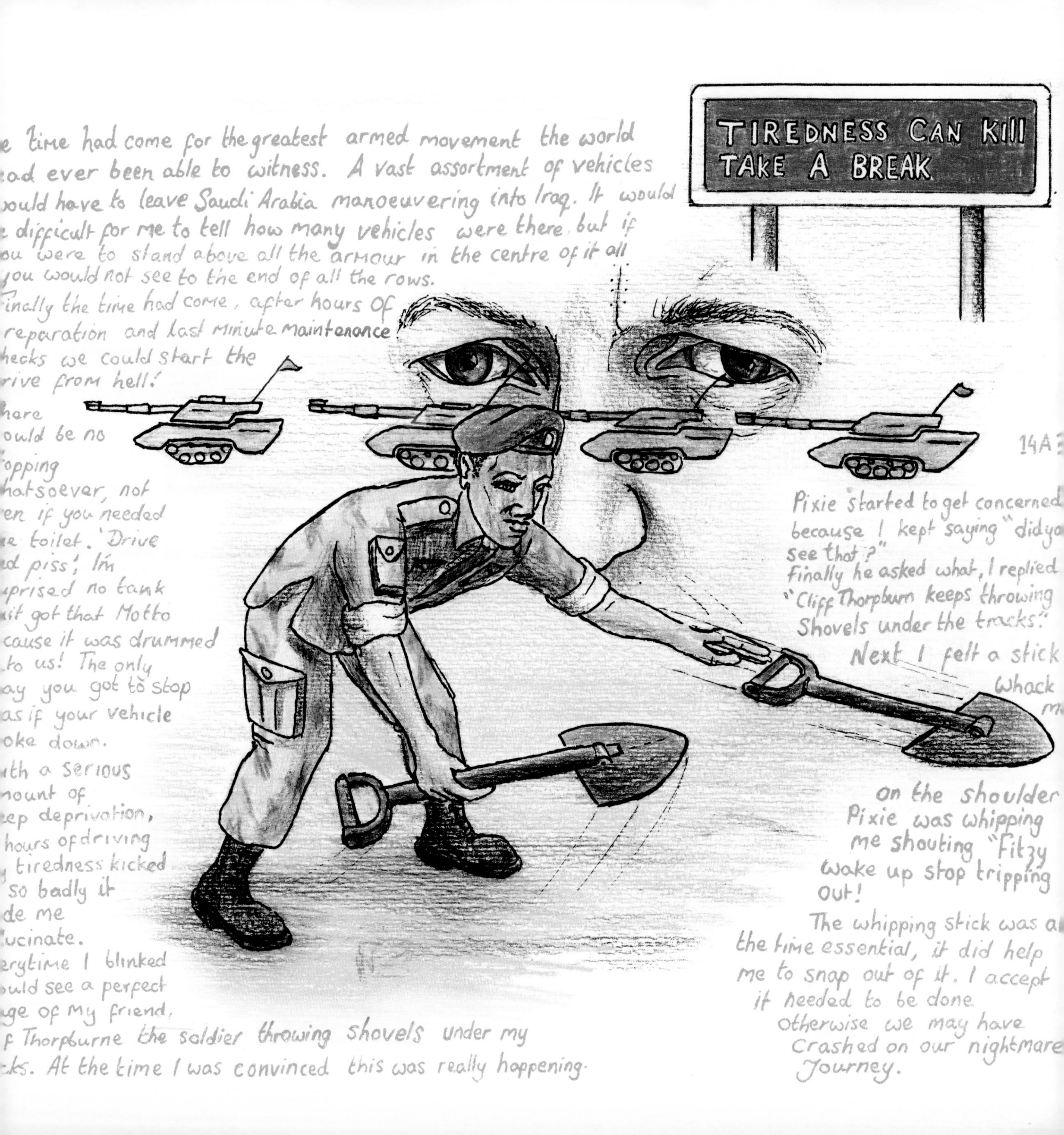
TIREDNESS CAN KILL
TAKE A BREAK
e time had come for the greatest armed movement the world
ad ever been able to witness. A vast assortment of vehicles
ould have to leave Saudi Arabia manoeuvering into Iraq. It would
difficult for me to tell how many vehicles were there, but if
ou were to stand above all the armour in the centre of it all
you would not see to the end of all the rows.
inally the time had come, after hours of
reparation and last minute maintenance
hecks we could start the
rive from hell!
here
ould be no
opping
hatsoever, not
en if you needed
e toilet. 'Drive
d piss', I'm
prised no tank
it got that Motto
cause it was drummed
to us! The only
ay you got to stop
as if your vehicle
oke down.
th a serious
nount of
ep deprivation,
hours of driving
tiredness kicked
so badly it
de me
ucinate.
erytime I blinked
ould see a perfect
ge of my friend,
f Thorpburne the soldier throwing shovels under my
ks. At the time I was convinced this was really happening.
14A
Pixie started to get concerned
because I kept saying "didyo
see that?"
Finally he asked what, I replied
"Cliff Thorpburn keeps throwing
Shovels under the tracks!"
Next I felt a stick
whack
m
on the shoulder
Pixie was whipping
me shouting "Fitzy
wake up stop tripping
out!
The whipping stick was a
the time essential, it did help
me to snap out of it. I accept
it needed to be done
otherwise we may have
crashed on our nightmare
journey.

The time had come for the greatest armed movement the world had ever witnessed. A vast assortment of vehicles would have to leave Saudi Arabia, manoeuvring into Iraq. It would be difficult for me to tell how many vehicles were there, but if you were to stand above all the armour in the centre of it you would not be able to see to the end of all the rows.

Finally the time had come. After hours of preparation and last minute maintenance checks we could start the drive from hell. There would be no stopping whatsoever, not even if you needed the toilet. 'Drive and piss': I'm surprised no tank unit got that motto because it was drummed into us! The only way you got to stop was if your vehicle broke down.

With a serious amount of sleep deprivation, after 18 hours of driving my tiredness kicked in so badly it made me hallucinate. Every time I blinked I could see a perfect image of my friend, Cliff Thorpburn, the soldier throwing shovels under my tracks. At the time I was convinced this was really happening.

Pixie started to get concerned because I kept saying, "Did you see that?" Finally he asked what and I replied, "Cliff Thorpburn keeps throwing shovels under the tracks."

Next I felt a stick whack me on the shoulder. Pixie was whipping me, shouting, "Fitzy wake up, stop tripping out!"

The whipping stick was at the time essential. It did help me snap out of it. I accept it needed to be done, otherwise we might have crashed on our nightmare journey.

Deserts may look flat but don't be deceived by the barren plains. It's like driving over waves and sometimes it can make you feel quite sea-sick. It's also easy to have an accident on such a bumpy surface, and I did.

Driving a vehicle so heavy can have no mercy when you take a bump wrong. The impact shakes the whole crew around like marbles rattling in a baked bean can. This accident hurt my back so badly that day that I had to stop driving. The pain got to me so I decided to take some pain killers.

All the crew were issued with mini first aid packs so I broke into mine. I found two sets of tablets in the box. One said Pain, the other said Severe Pain. To me pain is pain, so I took the Severe Pain option. Two pills knocked the balls out of me. They really tripped me out. All I could do was wander off and stare at the trippy lights on the tank (at the time they were beautiful).

My commander happened to notice I was acting strange, so he came over and asked what was going on. At first he went nuts at me after I told him what tablets I had taken. He told me that the ones I had taken were for the likes of gunshot wounds, and he also realised that I wasn't fit to drive. My commander decided it would be better if he drove that night. I got back to the vehicle and the commander strapped me to the stretcher and drove for the rest of the night. While he was driving, all I could do was trip out and laugh. All I could think was, 'What a rush!'

Tanks For The Memory

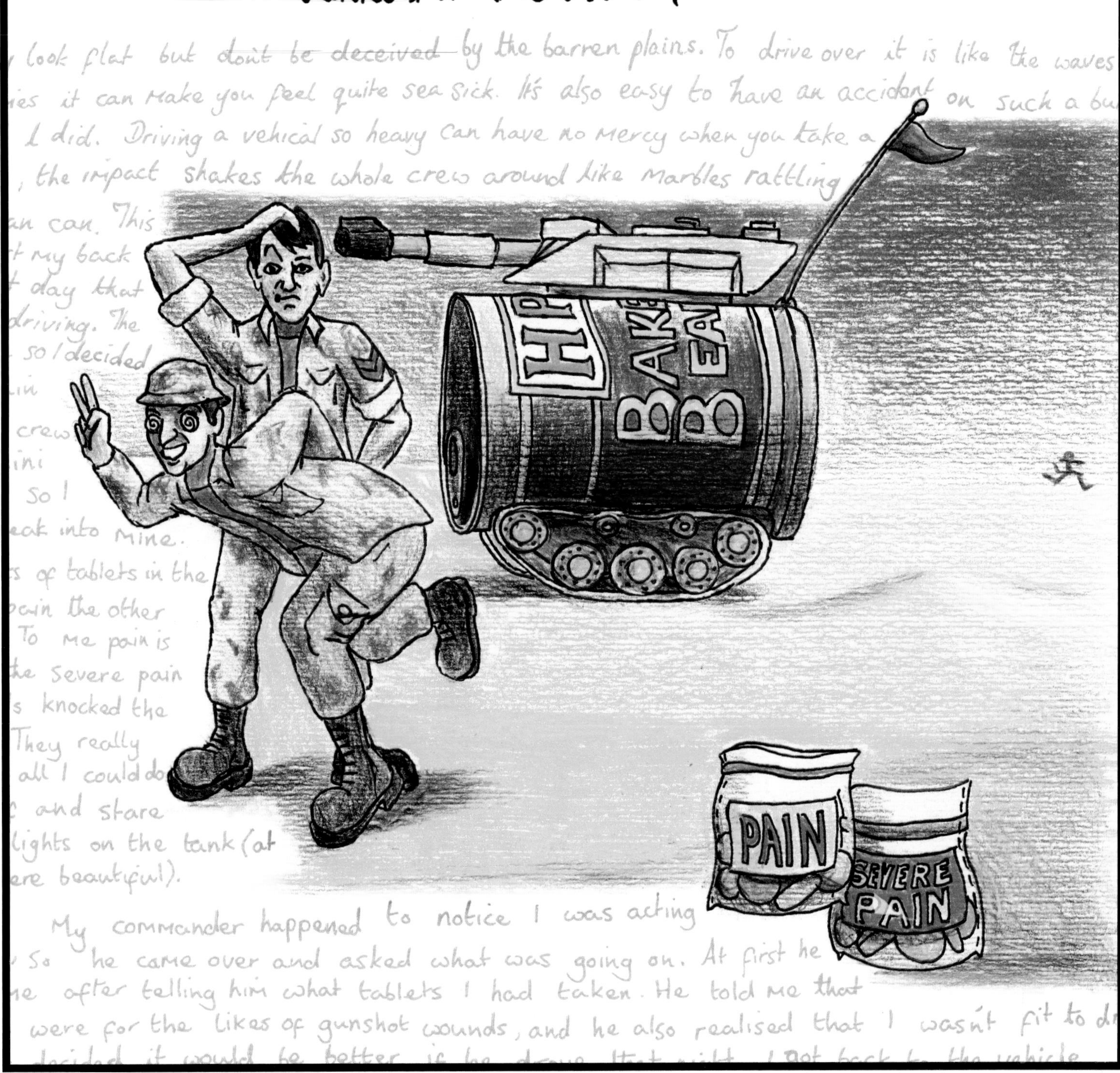

look flat but dont be deceived by the barren plains. To drive over it is like the waves
it can make you feel quite sea sick. It's also easy to have an accident on such a
I did. Driving a vehical so heavy can have no mercy when you take a
the impact shakes the whole crew around like marbles rattling
My commander happened to notice I was acting
he came over and asked what was going on. At first he
after telling him what tablets I had taken. He told me that
were for the likes of gunshot wounds, and he also realised that I wasn't fit to
HP
PAIN
SEVERE PAIN

CRUMBS

was quite happily driving towards Iraq and thinking about the the dangers of what w
approaching. So whilst being en route I will enjoy the safety and comfort of my vulnerable vehi
until I heard Pixie shout "Oh shit!" over the communications system.
what was wrong and he replied "Shit, shit, I was just checking
scorpion in the biscuit tin, then you hit a rut and I dropped
with the scorpion in it".
t now?" I urgently asked.
now, its somewhere in this
Pixie answered.
ing none of it, I hit
s straight away
t out of the
nd refused
ny further
scorpion
located.
dont mind
at but being
by a scorpion
the question.
the scorpion
d and
n, really
not want
p, not
much
n
w
here
ld be a
e tale!

Detect the Irony.
Shit I've dropped the Scorpion
BUSCOITS
Slight exaggeration
148

There I was, quite happily driving towards Iraq and thinking about the dangers of what we could be approaching. So while en route, I decided to enjoy the safety and comfort of my vulnerable vehicle (detect the irony).

That was until I heard Pixie shout, "Oh shit!" over the communications system. I asked what was wrong and he replied, "Shit, shit, I was just checking out the scorpion in the biscuit tin, then you hit a rut and I dropped the tin with the scorpion in it."

"Where is it now?" I asked urgently.

"I don't know, it's somewhere in this wagon," Pixie answered.

I was having none of it. I hit the brakes straight away and leapt out of the vehicle and refused to drive any further until the scorpion had been located. I thought, 'I don't mind being shot at but being taken out by a scorpion is out of the question.'

Eventually the scorpion was found and stamped on. Really, you would not want to pick it up, not after how much it had been annoyed. I always knew by going to this war there would be a sting in the tale!

Life can be pretty dull in the desert, especially if you live in and drive the squadron ambulance. However if you convert it into a mobile casino, things can become quite interesting, day and night. As soon as we parked up the cards came out. The games would commence for the select few, the ones with rank and known as the card sharks.

Looking at these I knew it wouldn't be long before I got roped in with them. This was the perfect place to learn a poker face. Being around the sharks was an expensive education so I spent more time with pissed-off face.

The only lucky thing in my game was we were never attacked during a card game. If we had been, the enemy would have really been in trouble!

Casinbulance

can be pretty dull in the desert, especially if you live in and drive the
dron ambulance. However if you convert it into a mobile casino things can
e quite interesting, day and night and as soon as we parked up the cards came out.
ames would commence for the select
he ones
ank and
as the
harks.
at
l knew
ldn't be
ore I got
with
is was
ct place to
oker face. Paying around
ks was an expensive
n So I spent more
h pissed off face.
ly lucky thing in my
was, we were never
ed during a card game
e the enemy would have
en in trouble!
Poker face Bob
14B
Ere, what do you think they get up to in there?

Close Encounter Of The Turd Kind
My first dump in the
desert, was a disaste
All I had to do w
dig a hole and then
bombs away, you
would think nothing
Could be more
simple?
What the?
There I was dumping away minding
My own business, until I heard a
rapid ticking noise. For a moment I
thought I might be sitting near an
accelerated time bomb, until
the noise started to get
Closer. Next I noticed
a big black thing
flying towards me,
Suddenly it landed
in my pants. In fright
I stood up rather rapidly, with
the log disconnecting into the
back of my overalls.
In panicking I
Somehow
Managed
to flick out, what a
dung beetle
After that
of my over
thought
The bee
and I had
tank with
Explain that
compo

My first dump in the desert was a disaster. All I had to do was dig a hole and then bombs away. You would think nothing could be simpler.

There I was, dumping away, minding my own business, until I heard a rapid ticking noise. For a moment, I thought I might be sitting near an accelerated time bomb, until the noise started to get closer. Next I noticed a big black thing flying toward me. Suddenly it landed in my pants. In fright, I stood up rather rapidly, with the log disconnecting into the back of my overalls. Panicking, I somehow managed to flick out what appeared to be a very large dung beetle, out of my pants.

After that, I shook the turd out of my overalls, looked at them and thought, 'Too messy', so I buried them. The beetle rolled away my log and I had to walk back to the tank with hardly any clothes on. Explain that one to the boys...

Sugar Bomb

Introducing Compo, The food of the British Forces that turns one's Faeces into that of a tyrannosaurus
Within the Army this food can be the equivalent to currency i.e. One tin of baby's heads (steak & kidney
pudding) = 2 tins of chicken curry, 1x chicken curry = 8 tins of cheese Possessed (Processed che
and 1 x tin of chocolate + boiled sweets + matches = an entire ration pack. However, this form of currency
holds no value unless you have the sacred key, the Sangreal, commonly
known as the trusty old tin opener...

mpo also shares a
ore sinister secret?
s this innocent
of food is
so a weapon of
ss destruction.
look at it
u would think
look at it, a
rmless tin of sugar
o sweet." Now
me tell you, in
e wrong hands
gives the
ing of
n a
of whoop ass" a
ole new meaning!

Compo Gourmet Recipe

1 x Oat meal biscuit
1 x Slice of Processed Cheese
1 x Dollop of Strawberry Jam
Stick em all togeather and bingo, a meal fit for a king / Queen...

s was demonstrated to me
worse throwing a tin of Sugar into the fire and shouting at me
..! After saying what? a few times I decided to run and take cover.
The tin exploded letting molten sugar explode everywhere. Ev
rtunately I didn't run fast enough. The tin exploded letting molten sugar explode everywhere. Ev
se for me I was wearing shorts at the time and the scorching sugar sprayed the back of my
amelising them. The pain was unbearable, but I did have the sweetest legs in the regiment.

Introducing Compo, the food of the British forces that turns one's faeces into that of a tyrannosaurus. Within the Army, this food can be the equivalent to currency, i.e. one tin of baby's heads (steak and kidney pudding) = 2 tins of chicken curry, 1 x chicken curry = 8 tins of cheese possessed (processed cheese) and 1 x tin of chocolate + boiled sweets + matches = an entire ration pack. However, this form of currency holds no value unless you have the sacred key, the Sangreal, commonly known as the trusty old tin opener...

Compo also shares a more sinister secret. Yes, this innocent tin of food is also a weapon of mass destruction. To look at it, you would think, 'Oh look, a harmless tin of sugar; how sweet.' Now let me tell you, in the wrong hands this gives the saying of 'open a can of whoop ass' a whole new meaning!

This was demonstrated to me by Tinker throwing a tin of sugar into the fire and shoting at me, "Run!" After saying, "What?" a few times, I decided to run and take cover. Unfortunately I didn't run fast enough. The tin exploded, spraying molten sugar everywhere. Even worse for me, I was wearing shorts at the time and the scorching sugar caught the back of my legs, caramelising them. The pain was unbearable, but I did have the sweetest legs in the regiment.

A quiet moment alone in the desert, that's all I needed. Just a little space. Sometimes it's too much to ask, especially when you have a commander like mine. Coming over to my space, he broke the silence, his first words being, "Hello you fat bastard" in a jokey way. My response to that in a jokey kind of way was to do some kind of judo throw on him. It looked and felt like a good idea until I heard a click and a scream. I didn't realise his foot was stuck in the sand and on twisting around awkwardly his knee popped and dislocated.

The next thing I knew, the medics had run over with a stretcher. They loaded my commander onto it. I went over to see if he was all right. He was well pissed off; looking at his face gave me the green light to give him some space. If only I could have turned back the clock, because from this I lost my commander for three months. I was gutted because this meant he would have to be replaced. For my sins, the replacement was to be a gung-ho officer. It was like a form of punishment in itself. The sooner my commander came back, the better – the replacement did my brain in!

The Twist...

quiet moment alone in the desert, that's all I needed just a little space. Sometimes it's
much to ask for, especially when you have a commander like mine. Coming over to my space
broke the silence his first words being "Hello you fat bastard" in a jokey way. My response
that in a jokey kind of way was to do some kind of Judo throw on him, it looked and felt like a
idea until
rd a click
scream. I
realise his
was stuck in
nd, upon
him around
rdly his
pped and
ed.
t thing
like
an over
stretcher
dad my
r on

Erm... You O.K.?

When I get back I'M going to kill you Fitzy you bastard!

to see if he was alright, he was well pissed off, looking at his face gave me
light to give him some space. If only I could have turned back the
cause from this I lost my commander for three months, I was gutted
this meant he would have to be replaced! For my sins the replacement
e a gung ho officer, it was like a form of punishment in itself.
ooner my commander come back the better, the replacement done my brain

Fitzy

He saved this bullet for me

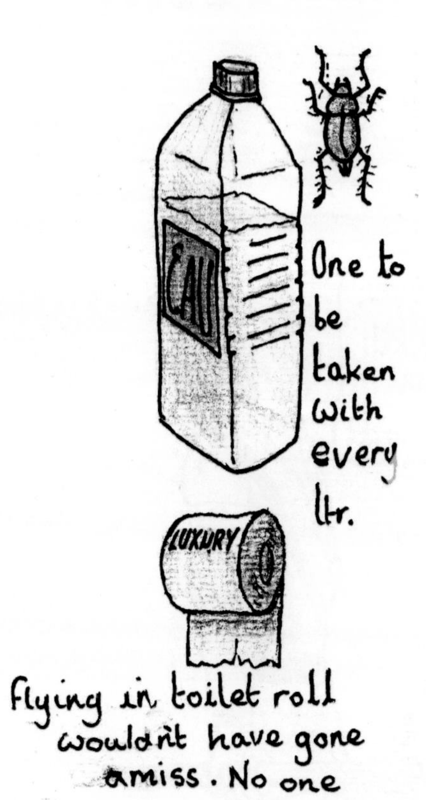

One to be taken with every ltr.

Flying in toilet roll wouldn't have gone amiss. No one ever shares it in the army. Get your own Stash!

There came a time in the desert when everyone caught D and V (diarrhoea and vomiting). This was to become an epidemic throughout the British Army, even to the point where Y-front pants had to be flown to the front line troops.

According to rumour control, the cause of this outbreak was my best friend, the dung beetle. Apparently the little turd roller drowned in the military's main water supply and caused absolute mayhem!

Life saving equipment: dispose of wisely.

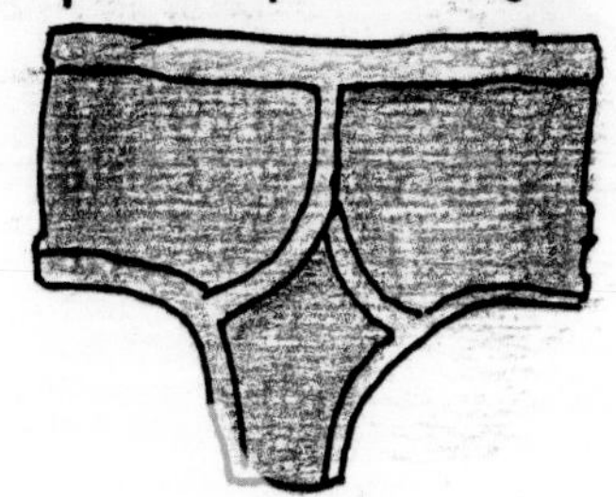

The Blue Pants Brigade
There came a time in the desert when everyone caught D.and V(Diarrhoea & Vomiting). This was to become an epidemic throughout the British Army, even to the point of where 'Y front pants had to be flown to the front line troops.
According to rumour Control the cause of this outbreak was due to my best friend the dung beetle. Apparently the little turd roller drowned in the military's main water supply and caused absolute mayhem!!!

30 Minutes In.
n't too long before we came across
rst casualty of war.
qi soldier had been shot
times by one of our tanks
s in need of urgent
on.
ob was to drive the
ed ambulance as
the casualty without
ourselves in any
, our main fear
e soldier
making
r the
itch up by
a ready
nate hand-
e. Ironic, just before trying to
his man's life you would need to
n in the groin, jump flat on his back, roll him
side whilst using his body as a blast shield
the booby trap.
ob was to get out of the vehicle and make safe the peripheral
checking for any other potential threats whilst the medics
to the wounded soldier. After making safe I would then
help the medics, who were diving straight into the job with
ete professionalism. I watched them cut and tear away at
atient's clothes revealing perfectly punctured flesh holes.
was no blood because the white hot bullets sealed the
upon penetration, looking at the holes nearly made me feel
Our patient's deep shock prevented hi
from making any noise. The medic co
see the pain in the soldier's face a
he dressed the wounds.
Our other Medic was at
same time trying
administer an intraveno
drip into the man's arm, th
was proving all too difficult
because the casualty's vei
had collapsed.
I remember hear
Staff Parkinson sa
to the other med
" If you can't f
the vein inse
the canula
anyway, thi
man needs f
before it's too
Finally we got the
Iraqi into the
Ambulance and w
then able to hea
the nearest fiel
hospital.
Whilst driving to the
hospital all I could t
was shit, if this is
the first half hour o
war looks like, w
it going to be like
the end of the day

It wasn't too long before we came across our first casualty of war. An Iraqi soldier had been shot several times by one of our tanks and was in need of urgent attention. Our job was to drive the armoured ambulance close to the casualty without putting ourselves in any danger, our main fear being the soldier could be making ready for the final stitch-up by lying on a ready-to-detonate hand grenade. Ironically, just before trying to save this man's life, you would need to kick him in the groin, jump flat on his back, roll him on his side while using his body as a blast shield against the booby trap.

My job was to get out of the vehicle and make safe the peripheral area, checking for any other potential threats while the medics tended to the wounded soldier. After making safe, I would then try to help the medics, who were diving straight into the job with complete professionalism. I watched them cut and tear away at the patient's clothes, revealing perfectly punctured flesh. There was no blood because the white hot bullets sealed the flesh upon penetration. Looking at the holes nearly made me sick...

Our patient's deep shock prevented him from making any noise. The medic could see the pain in the soldier's face as he dressed the wounds.

Our other medic was at the same time trying to administer an intravenous drip into the man's arm. This was proving all too difficult because the casualty's veins had collapsed. I remember hearing Staff Parkinson shout to the other medic, "If you can't find the vein insert the canula anyway. This man needs fluid before it's too late."

Finally we got the Iraqi into the ambulance and were then able to head to the nearest field hospital. While driving to the hospital, all I could think was, 'Shit, if this is what the first half hour of war looks like, what's it going to be like at the end of the day?'

The first thing I noticed upon arrival at the field hospital was the blood-soaked sand and the sea of casualties, and things weren't getting any better as we had another casualty to add to the list. Everyone working in this place really had their work cut out for them, and as much as everyone was rushing around trying to cater for every casualty, the doctors, nurses, medics and bandsmen were really doing an extraordinary job. I really do take my hat off to the bandsmen who are not only great musicians but people who are medically trained and work with all the other units on the front line tending to casualties under enemy fire. So never knock a Bandy!

Something that really came to my attention was 95 per cent of casualties were Iraqi soldiers, all injured, crying and some very close to dying. Seeing them so scared and trying to help everyone as well as each other really hit my human chord. Here before me were men who no longer seemed to be my enemy. Suddenly my indoctrinated hate towards these people subsided, making room for communication and compassion. This left me feeling quite confused, and I started to ask myself what the hell I was doing there? Was the liberation of Kuwait really worth all this pain and suffering?

Answer: Yes it was because there were innocent people who were still suffering.

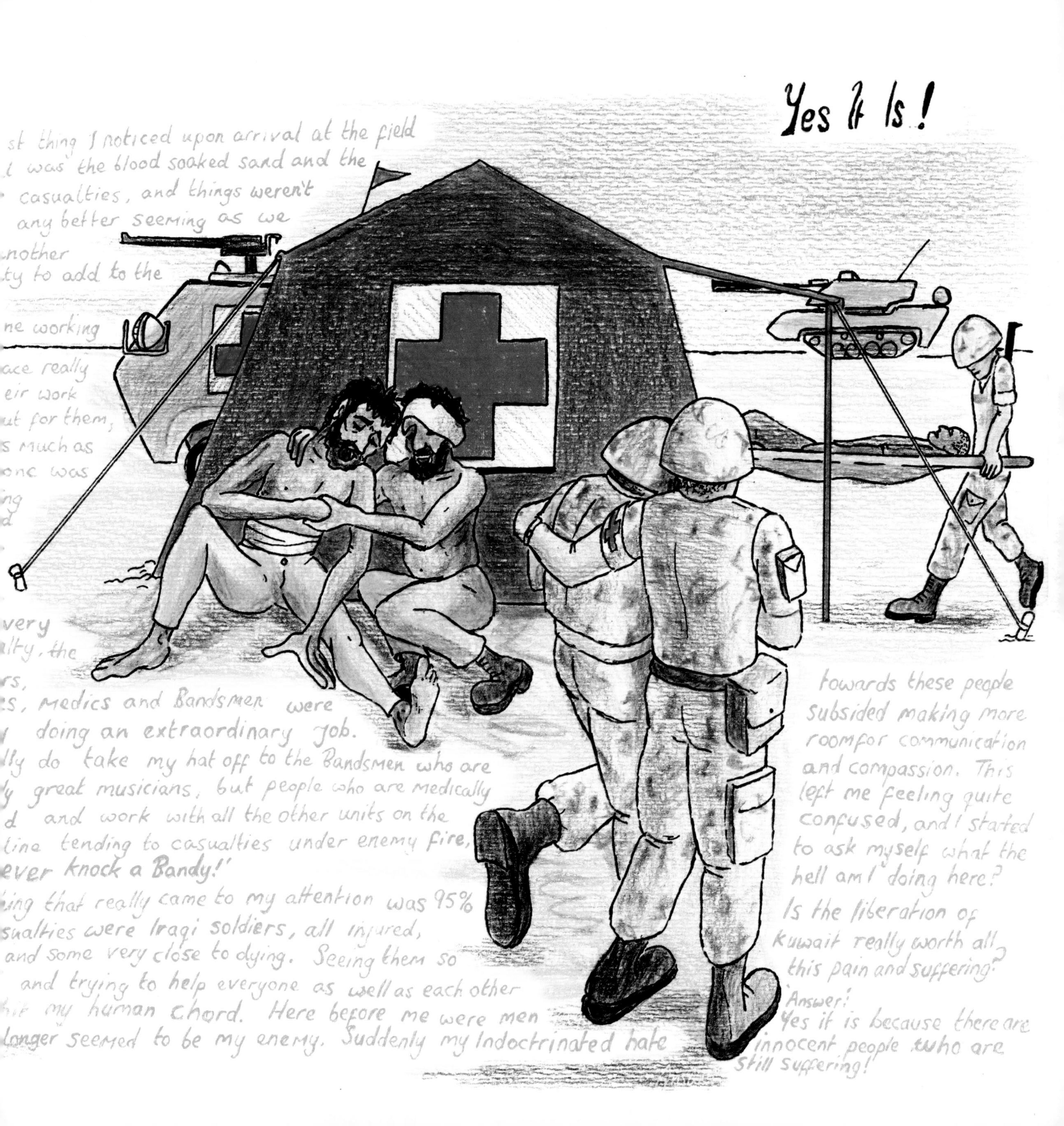
Yes It Is!
st thing I noticed upon arrival at the field
t was the blood soaked sand and the
casualties, and things weren't
any better seeming as we
nother
ty to add to the
ne working
ace really
eir work
ut for them,
s much as
one was
ng
d
very
lty, the
rs,
s, Medics and Bandsmen were
doing an extraordinary job.
lly do take my hat off to the Bandsmen who are
y great musicians, but people who are medically
d and work with all the other units on the
line tending to casualties under enemy fire,
ever knock a Bandy!'
ing that really came to my attention was 95%
sualties were Iraqi soldiers, all injured,
and some very close to dying. Seeing them so
and trying to help everyone as well as each other
hit my human chord. Here before me were men
longer seemed to be my enemy. Suddenly my Indoctrinated hate
towards these people
subsided making more
room for communication
and compassion. This
left me feeling quite
confused, and I started
to ask myself what the
hell am I doing here?
Is the liberation of
Kuwait really worth all
this pain and suffering?
Answer!
Yes it is because there are
innocent people who are
still suffering!

Now You See him, Now You Don't.

Radio transmission: "Sir, you are not going to believe this but we have just sighted an Iraqi soldier cycling across the desert with a rocket launcher on his back. What should we do?"

Sir: "Does he appear to pose a threat?"

Radio: "Well, he does have a rocket launcher!"

Sir: "Mmm. Well, if in doubt, take him out!"

Boom, only half a smoking bicycle was left.

Sometimes when I look back, I realise how lucky I am. There is nothing worse than feeling self pity. I don't know why but I keep remembering the hundreds of prisoners we had to search during the Gulf War.

Things really hit home for me when I searched a prisoner and all I could find was a half-eaten onion in his pocket, probably the most he had eaten for days. These people were all starved, weak and no longer had any fight left in them. After searching them, all we could do was leave them where we found them. They were all desperate to go home but there was nothing we could do because the war was still going on around us. I guess the most daunting thing was not knowing what would become of them once we had left the scene. All I knew was life would only get a lot harder for them.

I sometimes wonder how I could ever feel sorry for myself, knowing that I never had experienced life on half an onion. My problems are inferior to this but still I feel them.

CHECK SHALLOT

uess sometimes when I look back I realize how lucky I am. There is nothing worse then feeling self pity, I don't know why but I keep remembering the hundreds of prisoners we had to Search during the Gulf war. Things really hit home for me when I searched a risoner and all I could find was a half eaten onion in his pocket, probably the most he had eaten for days. These people were all starved, weak and no longer had any fight left in them. After searching them all we could do was leave them where we found them They were all desperate to go home but there was nothing we could do because the war was still going on around us. I guess the most daunting thing was not knowing what would become of them once we had left the scene, all I knew was life would only get alot harder for them.

I sometimes wonder at how I could ever feel sorry for myself knowing that I never had experienced life on half an onion. My problems are inferior to this but still I feel them!

Meet The Enemy
The latest addition to our crew
of war). Rather than leave him
him on board our wagon.
afraid,
gun at
he tried
Seeing
me
The only
Last eaten
Judging by the
for washing too.
fruit cocktail
personally I
glad to get
tasted like
began to feel
He introduced
Saddam. He asked if
Next he put his fingers to his
and asked if Saddam Hassien was
Sorry Mal, we forgot to tell you your gun wasn't loaded when you were guarding the p.o.w. Oops...

The latest addition to our crew was a stranded POW (Prisoner of War). Rather than leave him alone in the desert, we had to take him on board our wagon. At first our POW looked so afraid, understandable because I was pointing a gun at him. Fearing for his life, he tried to offer me his watch.

Seeing this man so petrified really put me in touch with my humane side again. The only way I could reassure him that he would be okay was to offer my hand out to him while introducing myself. Seeing this man had really been through the thick of the war, I asked him when he had last eaten. He told me a week ago, and judging by the smell it was about the same for washing too. I opened a tin of fruit cocktail and offered it to the POW. Personally I hated the stuff and was only too glad to get rid of it, but to him it must have tasted like heaven.

From this point the POW began to feel more at ease with our crew. He introduced himself to us, saying his name was Saddam. He asked if the war was over. I replied, "Yes." Next he put his fingers to his forehead in a gun-like gesture and asked if Saddam Hussein was dead. In embarrassment, we all said no. To my surprise, Saddam began to cry. It made me realise that this man didn't want to fight, he only ever wanted to be at home with his children.

This war was a complete failure. We failed to stop a tyrant. The only victory that may derive from this is Saddam going home and telling how he had met others who were humane and that there is still heart in this world.

The aftermath of war is not the most desirable thing to encounter. We came across a load of dead Iraqi soldiers. The sight was quite horrific. As much as these were the people that would have killed me if given a chance, I couldn't help but feel for them as fellow humans.

One caught my attention. He was the one that had died with his eyes open. I don't know why but I felt the compulsion to look into his eyes. They were dull with no reflection. The sparkle in the eye is what shows the soul. In this man, the soul was no longer there. To me, an everlasting image.

Other soldiers were gathering around to look at the museum of the dead. They were laughing and joking in the manner of pack instinct. Two soldiers really disgusted me. One was having a photo taken with his gun pointed towards the dead Iraqi's head, as if to say, 'Look how clever I am.' The other was even worse. He was actually removing a watch from another dead soldier's arm. This broke my heart: no respect. But still I laughed the crocodile way.

How Would you Feel?

you will end up dreaming about this one day..

Facing up to the aftermath of War is not the most desirable thing to encounter. We came across aload of dead Iraqi Soldiers, the sight was quite horrific. As much as these were the people that would have killed me if given a chance, I couldn't help but feel for them (fellow humans).

One Soldier caught my attention, it was the one that died with his eyes open. I don't know why but I felt the compulsion to look into his eyes, they were dull with no reflection. The sparkle in the eye is what Shows the Soul, in this Man the soul was no longer there. To Me an everlasting image!

Other soldiers were gathering around to look at the museum of the dead, they were laughing and Joking in the manner of pack instinct.

To my disdain there were two soldiers who really disgusted me. One was having a photo taken with his gun pointed towards the dead Iraqi's head, as if to say look how clever I am. The other was even worse. He was actually removing a watch from another dead soldier's arm, this broke my heart, no respect, but still I laughed the crocodile way.

It was a pleasant day, the war was over and I was doing my usual arguing with Pixie about something totally irrelevant, so everything was almost back to normal. That was until we heard a loud explosion and then could see a great cloud of smoke on the horizon. All of a sudden JB (another of our crew) appeared at the back of our ambulance, looking as white as a sheet. Puffing and panting, he shouted, "It's Billy, he's... he's... he's blown his leg off! Help!"

That instant we grabbed a stretcher and ran like hell to where the explosion had taken place. Finally we reached Billy who was lying on the ground, leg covered in blood and supporting his gaping wound. Funny, I expected Billy to be rolling around screaming. Instead he was the opposite: calm and quiet. He looked toward us and calmly asked, "Have you got any fags?" Before being carted off to hospital, Billy smoked his cigarette. The way he smoked it nearly made smoking look good for you.

So what happened? Billy and JB were off on a wander, probably in search of some memorabilia. Billy happened to stumble across an unexploded smart bomblet (something that looks like a pregnant dart). Billy couldn't resist picking up the dart and throwing it like Eric Bristow (the famous darts player, for those who weren't around in his heyday) at an old abandoned car. Unfortunately the bomblet exploded on impact, sending a shard into Billy's leg.

Billy's leg is still intact and works okay but he was left with a good scar to remind him.

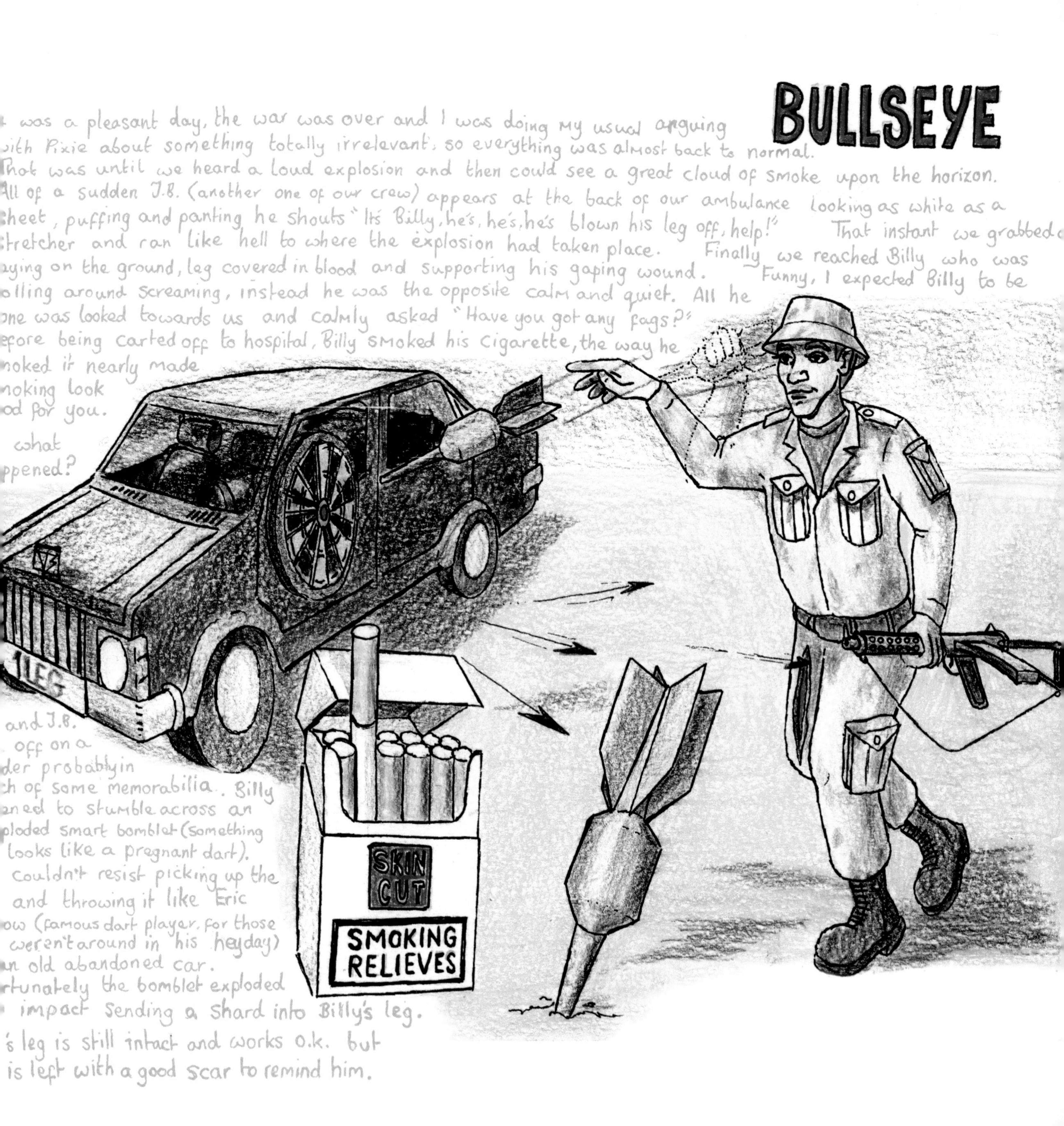
BULLSEYE
was a pleasant day, the war was over and I was doing my usual arguing
ith Pixie about something totally irrelevant, so everything was almost back to normal.
hat was until we heard a loud explosion and then could see a great cloud of smoke upon the horizon.
ll of a sudden J.B. (another one of our crew) appears at the back of our ambulance looking as white as a
heet, puffing and panting he shouts "It's Billy, he's, he's, he's blown his leg off, help!" That instant we grabbed
tretcher and ran like hell to where the explosion had taken place. Finally we reached Billy who was
aying on the ground, leg covered in blood and supporting his gaping wound. Funny, I expected Billy to be
olling around screaming, instead he was the opposite calm and quiet. All he
one was looked towards us and calmly asked "Have you got any fags?"
efore being carted off to hospital, Billy smoked his cigarette, the way he
noked it nearly made
noking look
od for you.
what
ppened?
and J.B.
off on a
der probablyin
h of some memorabilia. Billy
aned to stumble across an
ploded smart bomblet (something
looks like a pregnant dart).
couldn't resist picking up the
and throwing it like Eric
ow (famous dart player, for those
weren't around in his heyday)
n old abandoned car.
rtunately the bomblet exploded
impact sending a shard into Billy's leg.
's leg is still intact and works o.k. but
is left with a good scar to remind him.
11LEG
SKIN CUT
SMOKING RELIEVES

GRANDFATHER
ust as all units were put
stand by for the
lf War, my Grand-
her was taken
was ready for
ar but not ready
bad news like that.
equested compassionate
ve and was declined
on the notion that I may
t return to my regiment.
wever I was given an
imatum, I had to watch Sky
ws to see if our unit were
ng to war, if not I could
home and see my dying
andfather.
night mare came true
king at the t.v. my regimental
nbol appeared, twice my heart
s broken. Once for not being
le to see my Grandfather,
e other was for the lack of
st that I may not come back.
ound this an insult because
coward I am not!!!
WISH YOU WERE HERE
No one wrote to me to
my Grandfather had pa
while I lived in the vas
One night I looked to the
Saw a shooting star, fo
second It was like ha
Grandfather there with
As I watched the star d
into the night sky I kne
all by myself again.
Did he come to see me
The war finall
an end, time t
and celebrate o
return.
My bubble w
when I got
was told he
I was gone,
grandfather
away peace
I mentioned th
star to my fa
asked to be le
Although I was
for him, I beli
me a sign.

Just as all units were put on standby for the Gulf War, my Grandfather was taken ill. I was ready for war but not ready for bad news like that. I requested compassionate leave and was declined on the notion that I might not return to my regiment. However I was given a proposition. I had to watch Sky News to see if our unit was going to the war. If it wasn't, I could go and see my dying Grandfather.

My nightmare came true. Looking at my TV, the regimental symbol appeared. I could not believe my eyes. My colleagues cheered seeing this; I could not. Twice my heart was broken: once for not being able to see my Grandfather, the other for the lack of trust that I might not come back. I found this an insult because a coward I am not!

No one wrote to tell me my Grandfather had passed away while I lived in the vast desert. One night I looked to the sky and saw a shooting star. It was like having my Grandfather there with me. I watched that star disappear into the night sky. I knew I was all by myself again. Did he come to see me?

The war finally came to an end; time to go home and celebrate our victorious return. My bubble was burst when I got home and was told he had passed away peacefully while I was gone. I mentioned the shooting star to my family, then asked to be alone. Although I wasn't there for him, I believe he gave me a sign.

After coming out of the Gulf in one piece, you would have thought I would be an expert in the tank divisions. Far from it...

It was night time and I had to hang a camouflage net over my tank. Unfortunately for me, I slipped and landed astride the tank's dozer blade.

This really knocked the wind from my sails. Immediately I was rushed off to hospital to get my balls checked. To my relief, they were still there.

Swollen balls and laughing gas do not mix. Laughing on N2O made my balls feel like they were about to explode. The only bonus about the accident was I could pull a sicky and by jove I would milk that one! This was the start of a well deserved break.

Fact: This accident really hurt. Do not try this at home!

The Nut Cracker Soldier.
After coming out of the Gulf in one piece you would have thought I would be an expert in the tank division, far from it...
It was night time and I had to hang a camouflage net over my tank.
Unfortunately, especially for me, I slipped and landed astride the tank's dozer blade.
Erect barrel, I had no chance...
This really knocked the wind from my sails.
Immediately I was rushed off to hospital to get my balls checked. To my relief they were still there, swollen, but still there.
Swollen
balls
laughing
do not
laughing on
Made my
like they
to explode.
bonus about
accident was
pull a sicky
by jove I
Milk that
This was
of a
break.
Fact. This
not

Sweeny Todd
After the falling off the tank incident
and permanently being on light duties
my Sergent Major suggested to Me, to
ecome the
Regimental barber.
e knew I could
o this because
the amount
times I cut
is hair in the
ulf.
stantly I said
es but only if
e could arrange
room for Me,
needed salon
pace. The next
ay there it
as, my own
oom ready for
usiness, 'wicked!'
he next thing my Sergeant
Major said to me was
Fitzy, you're not allowed to
charge any more then £3.00.
asked who do I give
the money to at the
end of the day?
He said
That's your little side line,
here's one condition, you never
harge me, ever!'
Whose the poof now?
"Deal" I said try
out a big cheesey
What a result,
trooper with w
Office and ready for
what an achievem
rubbing my hands
The beauty of all
the every morning
if at the inspectio
hairy at the neck
Sent to me. This
position of power, e
needed me, Someti
because they had b
that they could pace
they didn't get the
Even the hierarch
my door asking
a trim, oh yeah
was on the oth
I did know what
me because if the
too high, I would
hair free of charge
like that
to
usep
This was like having an i
the regiment, no one wou
me just incase I fucked the

After the falling off the tank incident and permanently being on light duties, my Sergeant Major suggested that I become the regimental barber. He knew I could do this because of the number of times I had cut his hair in the Gulf. Instantly I said yes, but only if he could arrange a room for me. I needed salon space. The next day, there it was: my own room ready for business. Wicked.

The next thing my Sergeant Major said to me was, "Fitzy, you're not allowed to charge any more than £3."

I asked who I gave the money to at the end of the day. He said, "That's your little side line. There's one condition: you never charge me, ever!"

"Deal," I said, trying not to break out a big cheesy smile.

What a result. I was a trooper with an office and ready for business. What an achievement. I was rubbing my hands. The beauty of all this was that if, at morning parade, you were hairy at the neck, you were sent to me. This gave me a position of power; everybody needed me, sometimes desperately because they had been warned that they could face jail if they didn't get their hair cut. Even the hierarchy were at my door, asking politely for a trim. Oh yeah, the shoe was on the other foot!

I did know what was good for me because if the rank was too high, I would cut their hair free of charge. Favours like that would prove useful later on in life. This was like having an immunity in the regiment. No one would pick on me just in case I fucked their hair up.

Once upon a time, I believed that if you work hard, you party even harder. While we were away fighting in the Gulf War, a new movement, 'raving', had stormed its way across the UK. I honestly thought it was the best thing since sliced bread, but any movement would look good considering where I had just come from.

Raving also came with a mass subculture that coincided with the birth of the 'E' (MDMA). This was like the most amazing love drug ever. To me, this sounded quite appealing and like a very good form of escapism. I needed to let my hair down and leave the bad times behind me.

Raving really amazed me. The partying was great and although drug induced, the people I met were fantastic and showed nothing but love. It was like everyone on 'E' was completely liberated and really alive with the music that was immersing the surrounding environment. You could feel the tunes and love happening around you. That is what, at the time, I thought every squaddie should experience after the war.

I could not help taking an instant liking to this movement. Yes, I was hooked and loved it. To be honest, it was the downfall of my career in the Army. After my great introduction to raving, I went back to the regiment with the attitude of a hippy. It was like I found myself, like so many others at the time. Not recommended if you want a career. "Oi oi..."

Introducing
pon a time I believed that if you
ard you party even harder!
we were a
new mov
its way across the U.k.
tly thought it was the best thing
liced bread, but any movement
considering where
st come from!
also came
ass
re
ncided
e birth
E.
d
ppealing
e a very
orm of
sm, I needed
my hair down
eave the bad
behind me...
Raving really amazed
partying was great
drug induced the p
were fantastic and
nothing but love. It
everyone on E was
liberated and re
with the music tha
should exp
the war...
I could not
an instant
this movement
was hooked
to be honest
downfall of m
the army.
great introd
raving I went
regiment with t
a hippy, it was
myself, like somany others
Not recommended if you want a co

DREAMS, LIKE ALL GOOD AND WELL LOVED TOYS, CAN BECOME

DREAMS, LIKE ALL GOOD AND WELL LOVED TOYS, CAN BECOME

WORN AND BROKEN. REPAIR THE TOY. RESTORE THE PASSION.

Welcome Back To Society!

The day after leaving the Army, I went to the job centre to make a fresh claim. I had to queue for hours due to having a lot of people from my old area in front of me so it felt a bit like a reunion at the dole office. Eventually I made it to the desk where I encountered this woman who was eyeing me up and down and had a face like thunder – obviously all the locals had got to her. I could not help noticing her mug had 'Bitch' written on it. This intimidated me even more.

I politely told her I had just left the Army and needed help. What had I done? This woman said to me in an ill tone while rolling her eyes, "What did you leave the Army for? You had a roof over your head!"

Yes, the mug said it for me...

Without blowing a gasket, I explained my reasons (including the Gulf War big time) for leaving. This didn't even perturb her. All she said was, "I still don't see the reason why you left a perfectly secure job."

Next she gave me a mountain of forms and said, "Fill them in and bring them back to Box 2 next week."

How I never lost it I do not know. So much for a welcome back to society. This cow made me regret fighting for this country. What system did I fight for?

In Gravesend, work was getting a bit thin on the ground and I hadn't done any for quite a while either. This was causing quite a bit of boredom, leaving me set to do anything that might come my way. Something did!

A friend of mine, Nursey (a.k.a. Dave), had been working abroad and had come home for the weekend. In that weekend, he managed to convince me to go abroad and work with him as a tarmac layer. After agreeing, I asked, "Who are we working for?"

"Just a few chavs – they're all right. You get used to them," Dave replied in a not too convincing manner. "Go home, pack your bags and meet me outside the KFC tomorrow."

It was noon the next day and I was off to meet Nursey at the Kentucky. I was nervous and excited at the same time. I caught Nursey's eye at the meeting point and shouted, "Where's our ride then?" Nursey pointed to a load of vans with caravans attached and then said, "Here come the chavs right now!"

I couldn't believe it. By chavs I thought he meant a bunch of scummy people. We were off to work for a bunch of real gypsies. All I could think was, 'What have I let myself in for?' It was too late to back out. The van had just pulled up to us and a gypsy with a large uni-brow leaned out the van window, looked Nurse and me up and down and then said, "Get in boy!"

The next thing we were on our way to the south of France. This was going to be one long journey and it was going to be very slow because of the caravan attached. No one spoke apart from the uni-browed gypsy known as 'John boy' who loved the sound of his own voice. There was no conversation. It was all just foul mouth and swearing. All I could do was nod like I understood what the hell he was on about. Fourteen hours with a load of "inits": by the end of the journey I was ready to kill. All I could think was, 'This is the first day, God only knows what lies ahead.'

kin Gipsies

In Gravesend work was getting a bit thin on the ground and I hadn't done
any for quite a while either, so this was causing quite a bit of boredom therefore
leaving me set to do anything which might come my way, something did! A friend of mine (Nur
had been working abroad and had come home for the weekend, in that weekend he managed to
convince me to go abroad and work with him as a Tarma .. Upon agreement I asked
are working for ?"
Just a few chavs, they're alright
you use to them". David replied
in a not too convincing
manner, then Dave added
"Go home pack your bags
and meet me outside
the K.F.C. tomorrow!"

A.K.A.

They're Proper gipsys ?

Did'nt I tell you ?

was noon the next day
nd I was off to meet Nursey at the
entucky, I was nervous and excited at the same time, I caught Nursey's eye at the meeting
nd then shouted "where's our ride then ?" Nursey pointed to a load of Vans with caravans
ttached and then said "here come the Chavs right now!"
couldn't believe it, by Chavs I thought he meant a bunch of scummy people, I couldn't believe
were off to work for a bunch of real gipsies all I could think was what have I let myself in for
t was too late to back out and the Van had just pulled up to us, a gipsy with a large Uni-bro
hen leaned out of the Van window, looked Nurse and I up and down and then said "get in Boy!"
The next thing we were on our way to the south of France, this was going to be one long journe
and it was going to be very slow because of the caravan attached. No one spoke apart from t
Uni browed gipsy known as 'John boy' who loved the sound of his own voice, there was no conversation
was all just foul mouth and swearing, all I could do was nod like I understood what the hell h
was on about. 14 hours with a load of "Inits", by the end of the journey I was ready to kill, all I cou
was this is the first day God only knows what lays ahead!

long and tedious drive to the south of France, I finally met
ipsies I would be working for. No rest for the wicked, as soon
my friend Nursey introduced me to the head honcho Gipsy
s I put my hand out to shake John boy's hand, all he did was
unch of keys pointed to a lorry and said " Go on boy you're
!"
elieve it, this guy does not even know me but he hands the
assive
hat's

licence,
, its like
s a doddle,
can do it, gaw on!"

intimidated by this big
ing stuck in a situation
get out of I took the
d " What if I get stopped?
rs " Just show the
cence, it's written
o they won't
, you'll be o.k.!"
ht so I jumped in
quickly thought big
e it like one. All I
as 'Oh shit this is fun'

L
QUICK
Not too sure about th
Come on you can do it, gaw on!
85
RINGER L
P.S. All I could do is pray n to crash

After a very long and tedious drive to the south of France, I finally met the firm of gypsies I would be working for. No rest for the wicked. As soon as I arrived, my friend Nursey introduced me to the head honcho gypsy John Boy. As I put my hand out to shake John Boy's hand, all he did was give me a bunch of keys, pointed to a lorry and said, "Go on boy, you're driving that."

I could not believe it. This guy does not even know me but he hands the keys of a massive lorry to me. What's the story then?

"I haven't got a licence for that," I said.

John Boy instantly replied, "Yeah, but you got a driver's licence. Just drive it, it's like a big car. It's a doddle. Come on, you can do it. Gaw on!"

Feeling quite intimidated by this big guy and feeling stuck in a situation that I couldn't get out of, I took the keys and said, "What if I get stopped?"

John Boy answered, "Just show the frogs your licence. It's written in English so they won't understand it. You'll be okay."

'Sod it,' I thought, so I jumped in the lorry, thought 'big car' and drove it like one. All I could think was, 'Oh shit, this is fun.'

My first day working with the gypsies I couldn't believe my eyes and ears. I have never witnessed a bunch of cowboys like it. Everyone had their own little job to do, I swear I got the bum deal because my allocated jobs were truck driver, bitumen distributor and main shoveller. God it was hard work. The only person with the good job in this outfit was the roller man, a guy that would not help anyone no matter how hard you were struggling.

I honestly don't think we ever did a proper job. Sometimes the tarmac was laid so thin that it would come up with the roller wheels. Another job I inherited was to patch over where the roller messed up by running after the roller with a can of bitumen. I would fill in the holes and then quickly gravel over the top of it as recommended by my bosses.

As soon as the job was done, our bosses would collect the money. Then we would pack up fast and leg it to our next destination. I didn't like the job we were doing; at the time we had to, otherwise we would be stranded.

Some of our jobs were that bad the local mayors phoned all the other towns to warn them we were coming. How we never got tarred and feathered by the locals I will never know.

Wrong Road

My first day working for the gipsies I couldn't believe my eyes, ears and Job, I have never witnessed a bunch of cowboys like it. Everyone had their own little Job to do, I swear I got the bum deal because my allocated Jobs were truck driver, bituman distributer, and main shoveller, God it was hard work.
The only person with the good Job in this outfit was the roller man, a guy that would not help anyone no matter how hard you may be struggling!!!
I honestly don't think we ever done a proper Job. Sometimes the tarmac was laid so thin that it would come up with the roller wheels.
Another job I in
was to patch ove
the roller messe
running after the
with a can of bit
next I would fill in
holes and then qui
gravel over the to
as recommended
bosses.
As soon as th
was done ou
bosses would
the money,
we would pa
fast and le
our next
desti
I didn't
the job
doing, a
time we
otherwise w
Stranded!
Some of our Jobs were that bad even the local mayor phoned all the other local towns to warn them we were coming! How we never got tar and feathered by the locals I will never k

Hit
RUN
THAT WILL TEACH YA!
BANG
"There's got to be a gap in the fucking traffic by now?" Nursey Shouts anxiously getting impatient.
"Just hold on a second Someone will let us out soon?" I replied subtly trying to calm Nursey's road rage down.
"Fuck it, I'll let myself out!" Nursey said putting the Van into gear and rapid pulling out.
BANG
The man of great anger just hit a car and it was loud, all I could think as I was turning around to look at Nursey was "Good, that will show you for getting impatient and thinking you can do what you want!"
LEG IT
WHAT SHOULD I DO
REVERSE
Mean while there was a flock of French people gathering around the Van, even worse the driver of the other Vehical had arrived and was knocking on the Van door. In all the commotion Nursey panicing rolled up the window and rapidly drove off, now we were hit and runners, could it get any worse?
Somehow we got away with it?

"There's got to be a gap in the fucking traffic by now," Nursey shouted anxiously, getting impatient.

"Just hold on a second, someone will let us out soon," I replied, subtly trying to calm his road rage.

"Fuck it, I'll let myself out!" Nursey said, putting the van into gear and pulling out.

Bang! The man of anger hit a car and it was loud. All I could think as I was turning around to look at Nursey was, 'Good, that will show you for getting impatient and thinking you can do what you want.'

Meanwhile, there was a flock of French people gathering around the van. Even worse, the driver of the other vehicle had now arrived and was knocking on the van door speaking a language neither of us understood. In all the commotion, Nursey panicked, rolled up the window and rapidly drove off. Not only were we driving a bright yellow van with English number plates, we were now hit-and-runners.

Somehow we got away with it!

After the great hit and run incident, we told our bosses what actually happened and they warned us that we could not go back to the hotel in case our registration had been reported to the police and they were looking for us. One of the gypsies suggested they buy us a tent and we stay on the holiday resort with them rather than go to a hotel where we could be easily found. For fear of being caught, we agreed, although Nursey was not too forthcoming at first but understood this was the only way to get out of a sticky situation.

Nursey had never camped before. He always insisted on being hotelman. Our agreement was to camp on the other side of the resort because we didn't want to work and sleep with our bosses. They agreed, so we pitched our new tent.

The camp was excellent with life buzzing around us. This made our past hotels look like non-atmospheric places. Camping was very much the way forward; even Nursey agreed it was paradise. It was wicked and we were meeting loads of cool new people, and now finally we were ending up at beach parties every night. I have to admit the accident was the best thing that could have happened to us.

The Best Things Are Never Planned

reat hit and run incident we told our bosses what actually happened, and they warned
can not go back to the hotel in case our registration was reported to the police and they could be
us. One of the gipsies suggested they buy us a tent and we stay on the holiday resort with
er then go to a hotel where
be easily found.
ar of being caught
, although Nursey
o forthcoming
but understood
the only
et out of
ituation!

d never camped before he always insisted on being hotelman.
ement was to camp on the other side of the resort because
t want to work and sleep with our bosses. They agreed so
ed our new tent, the camp was excellent with life buzzing
s. This made our past hotels look like non-atmospheric places.
was very much the way forward, even Nursey agreed it was
. It was wicked and we were meeting loads of cool new people,
finally was ending up at beach parties every night. I got to
e accident was the best thing that could have happened to us!

GOOD WORK

ity of our work was mainly driveways (typical Gipsy trait, the old chestnut "I've got a
ft over from my last Job, I can do your driveway for very cheap") and alot of our Jo
eyards. The patrons knew this would be a gipsy Job, unbelievably they would still go ah
Some patrons even believed if
a few bottles of their
ne it might convince the
workers
tter
hem.
roblem
as was
s were
they
t even
er for
kers.
r accounted
heat from
c and the
nally hot
, that it
ydrating their work force.
itality was noted so our only option for getting
id was to drink the wine we stashed in the van,
, warm rosé is not recommended for taste but in
imate any form of rehydration was very welcome
t aware at the time that alcohol dehydrates). Just to add more salt, I will
wine gets to the brain alot quicker, funny but we would be completely pissed by
the Job. I do not condone drink driving or drink working, but to tell the tru
make the Job alot more interesting, and believe it or not we actually di
Job!

The majority of our work was driveways (typical gypsy trait, the old chestnut 'I've got a load of gear left over from my last job, I can do your driveway very cheap') and a lot of our jobs were vineyards. The patrons knew this would be a gypsy job; unbelievably they would still go ahead with it. Some patrons even believed if they gave a few bottles of their finest wine, it might convince the recipient workers to do a better job for them. Their hospitality was noted.

The only problem with this arose because our bosses were so tight they would not even buy water for their own workers. They never accounted for the heat from the tarmac and the exceptionally hot weather, that it was dehydrating their work force. So our only option for getting any liquid was to drink the wine we had stashed in the van.

Trust me, warm rosé is not recommended for taste but in that climate any form of rehydration was very welcome (I was not aware at the time that alcohol dehydrates). Just to add more salt, I will say warm wine gets to the brain a lot quicker. Funny but we would be completely pissed by the end of the job. I do not condone drink-driving or drink-working, but to tell the truth, it did make the job a lot more interesting. And believe it or not, we actually did a better job.

Spain: The setting could not be any more perfect. An empty beach at night, a magical full moon and a beautiful woman to make love to. It was all so breath-taking, it was like living in a dream.

That dream soon turned into a nightmare. While we were in the sea throwing passion at each other, some bastard was stealing our stuff. My girlfriend's bag was stolen and all my money and mobile was stolen from my jeans. All that was left were our clothes and a packet of cigarettes. Amazingly the thief stole the cigarettes from the packet but left us with two cigarettes and a lighter in the packet.

Being robbed somewhat burst our bubble, in fact it ruined the moment until we actually realised it could have been worse. Yes, the robber could have taken all the cigarettes. How thoughtful: it was like he knew that we would need a cigarette after. It almost cheered us up before going home.

Considerate Crime

ain
e setting could not be any more perfect, an
npty beach at night, a magical full moon, and
beautiful woman to make love to. It all was so
eath taking, it was like living in a dream.

t dream soon turned into a nightmare. While we were in the sea throwing passion at each othe
ne bastard was stealing our stuff. My girlfriend's bag was stolen and all my money and mobile
s stolen from my Jeans. All that was left was our clothes and a packet of cigarettes. Amazing
thief stole the cigarettes from the packet but left us with two cigarettes and a lighter in
packet. Being robbed somewhat burst our bubble infact it ruined the moment until we actuallu
lised it could have been worse, yes the robber could have taken all the cigarettes. How thoughtful

MUG
ke a short cut in the Costa Del Sol, I did and I came unstuck. I decided to walk
n alley which led directly to the next bar I was heading to, silly me I should have
e attention to the gang that was waiting for terribly drunk people like me to go up i
alf way up the alley this gang surrounded me and went into frisk mode, there were hands
e, yes I was being robbed.
these guys
hey wanted
ran off
r mate
pinned
wall behind
well
lifes.
pulling me
and telling
go and
es, it's all
that I could have

Never take a short cut in the Costa del Sol. I did, and I came unstuck. I decided to walk through an alley which led directly to the next bar I was heading to. Silly me. I should have paid more attention to the gang that was waiting for terribly drunk people like me to go up it.

As I got halfway up the alley, this gang surrounded me and went into frisk mode. There were hands everywhere. Yes, I was being robbed.

As soon as these guys got what they wanted, they quickly ran off, leaving their mate who I had pinned against the wall. For a second I thought my hurting this fellow might bring the others back with my stuff. Some friends: they left this one well behind, low lifes.

The next thing I remember is my friend Baz pulling me off this guy and telling me to let it go and cut my losses, it's all I could do. I suppose it could have been worse. I do realise I could have been stabbed or worse, but I do wish that I had bashed up the fellow a little bit more, a kind of message for his so-called mates.

After having a great night out in Fuengirola, I decided I wanted some fresh air and a nice stroll home. Stepping out from the nightclub into a nice quiet street felt like tranquility. I admit I was very drunk at the time and was having a right stagger on the way home. That was until two Spanish guys jumped me and started punching and kicking me. I don't know why but this sobered me up instantly (I think it was the kick in the face that did it). My instinct told me to get up and, no matter what, to fight back!

As I started getting to my feet, these two guys started beating me even harder. My fear was gone; they were hurting me but I did not care. I just thought, 'No more, that's it, I've had enough of being robbed out here. It's not going to happen this time!'

Finally I was on my feet and at eye level with the guy who had kicked me in the face. As soon as we made eye contact I let this punch rip. It was a beauty because it knocked him right out. One down, one to go. By this time I was kind of enjoying the fight. The other fellow looked stunned at what I had just done and looked even more worried because he knew he was next, so before I could get to him, he ran off. I gave chase but had too much booze in me to continue.

Ironically, about one minute after the fight my friends arrived at the scene. Looking at my blood covered face, they asked what had happened. I explained and all they said was, "Why didn't you wait for us?" My answer was, "Sod's law!"

SOD'S LAW

having a great night out in Fuengirola, I decided I wanted some fresh air and a
home. After a loud night out, stepping out from the night club onto a nice quiet st
like tranquility. I admit I was very drunk at the time (a bit like how my writing can be some
was having a right stagger on the way home, that was until two Spainsh guys jumped
started punching and kicking me. I don't know why but this sobered me up instantly, (I think
k in the face that done it) my instinct told me to get up and, no matter what, fight back!!!
started getting to my feet
two guys started beating
ven harder, my fear was
they were hurting me but
ot care. I just
ht 'no more
it I have
enough of
robbed out
it's not
to
en this time.
y I was on my
and at eye level
the guy who had
me in the
. As soon as
ade eye
ct I
his punch
t was a beauty
se it knocked him right out.
own one to go, by this time I was kind of enjoying the fight.
other fellow looked stunned at what I had just done and looked even more
d because he knew he was next so before I could get to him he run off.

I gave chase
had too much
in me to cont
Ironic, about c
minute after
fight my frie
arrived at th
scene. Look
at my blood
covered fa
they aske
happened,
explained
all they said
"why didn't yo
wait for us
My an
was: "Sod

You get out of life what you put in. Eventually I could see that getting stoned every day while on the dole was a dead end. I saw the change in a friend who had gone back to college. He was a different person and he was going places. So I enrolled to study art, and got aboard the onwards and upwards curve. You get out of life what you put in. Eventually I could see that getting stoned every day while on the dole was a dead end. I saw the change in a friend who had gone back to college. He was

a different person and he was going
places. So I enrolled to **study art** and
got aboard the onwards and upwards
curve. You get out of life what you put
in. Eventually I **could see** that getting
stoned every day while on the dole was
a **dead end**. I saw the change in a friend
who had gone back to college. He was a
different **person** and he was going
places. So I **enrolled** to study art. and
got aboard the onwards and **upwards**
curve. You **get out** of life what you put
in. Eventually I could see that getting

keep Learning
iend John suggested that we
get out of the situations
ere living in. John was
unhappy being a bus driver
eing on the dole getting
everyday was really
raining for me. I hated the
I had got myself into
anted out. After
about how much we
our lives
ally agreed
ack into
ion and
art.
friend of
Marcus) who
one this the
efore
anged
We
ee the
on,
like
ude
lude
e change
mazing
e was
to go
, and
nted
I got to admit I wa
to this environmen
insecure about m
because I was
School and th
helped either
dog that had
So I may hav
Volatile when
What changed
when I started
working so ho
before. I think
the same em
without the a
This was so more
encouragement
put me into
and alm
the err
As much
doing well
side of th
side was
when it
art his
knowle
Even th
approachi
we reass
D
D
F
MUM

My friend John suggested that we should get out of the situations we were living in. John was totally unhappy being a bus driver, and being on the dole getting stoned every day was really life draining for me. I hated the position I had got mself into and wanted out.

After talking about how much we hated our lives, we finally agreed to go back into education and study art. Another friend, Marcus, who had done this the year before, had changed totally. We could see the transition. It was like from rude boy to dude boy. The change was amazing. He was starting to go places and we wanted a slice. So we went to college trying to take onboard everything...

I have to admit I was struggling to adapt to this environment. I was a bit insecure about my intelligence because I was always put down at school and the Army had not helped either. I was a mad dog that had experienced death so I may have been a bit volatile when starting education.

What changed my life around was getting praised for working so hard. I never had that before. I think John was experiencing the same emotions as me but without the Army bit thrown in. This was so morale boosting. The encouragement at college really put me into another dimension and almost made me see the error of my ways.

As much as John and I were doing well with the practical side of things, the written side was a struggle, especially when it came to A-level art history. Our local knowledge let us down a bit. Even the lecturer was shy approaching us with this. We reassured him it was okay, we'd caught the education bug, nothing to fear because it was all onwards and upwards from there on in...

Art school was a very confusing time for me. There was no right formula for art, so how could anyone know if they were doing it right? When I was student rep, I asked at an official meeting how one could achieve a first. The reply I got was, "Those who get a first deserve a first." From there on in, I realised the whole criteria was made out of bullshit.

Everything I tried to do was always discouraged by our lecturers; funny, I thought higher education was about encouragement. I would take advice from one lecturer only to be told it was wrong by another. Apparently this was constructive criticism, a polite way of saying 'don't give up your day time job'.

I tried everything on advice. I minimalised, deconstructed, reconstructed and nearly self destructed. Basically, I spent four years discovering that I was on my own. I would call this a great journey of self discovery. The solution: stand on your own two feet and do what you feel is right and be the best at what you do... do it! No lecturer can tell you your heart is wrong.

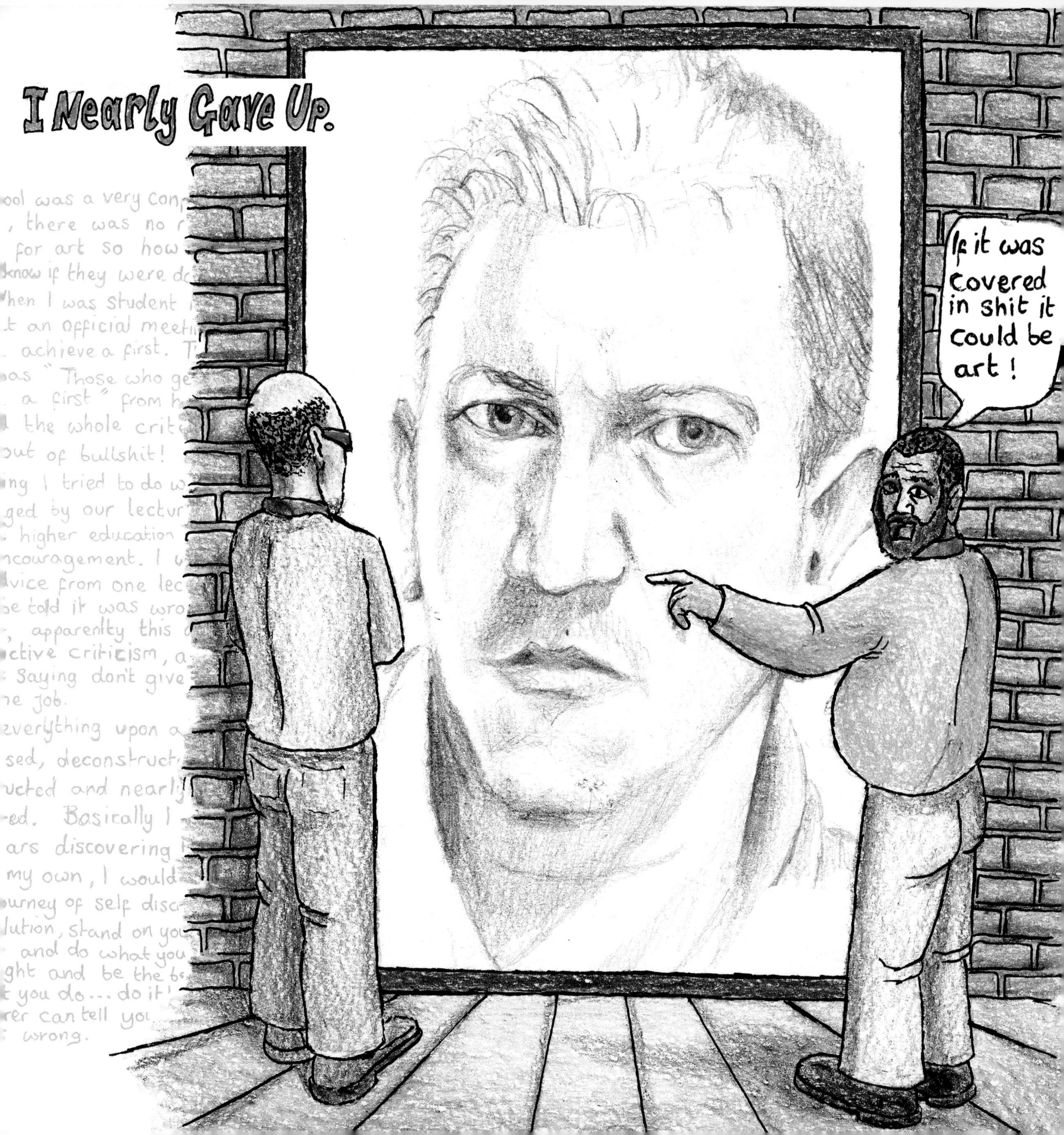
I Nearly Gave Up.
ool was a very comp
, there was no r
for art so how
know if they were d
hen I was student
t an official meeti
achieve a first. T
as "Those who ge
a first" from h
the whole crit
out of bullshit!
ng I tried to do w
ged by our lectur
higher education
ncouragement. I
vice from one lec
be told it was wro
, apparently this
ctive criticism, a
Saying don't give
e job.
verything upon a
sed, deconstruct
ucted and nearly
ed. Basically I
ars discovering
my own, I would
urney of self disc
lution, stand on yo
and do what you
ght and be the b
t you do... do it!
er can tell you
wrong.
If it was covered in shit it could be art!

Cultured

admit I was a bit like a mad dog when I started Art school, to tell the truth
ny insecure nature towards education that made myself a little volatile. My experience of
. not give me the confidence I needed towards further education, I guess this could be put do
nstant being told I was thick by teachers and pupils, eventually you end up believing it yoursel
in a nutshell I no longer
be the subject of
fter being exposed
nd becoming quite
my fighting ability,
o myself that I
longer be mentally
lly bullied. Kind of
attitude for further
I know, but this
did give me the
to put my foot
e door!
tional environment
anything that I
to expect from School,
was starting to get praise,
that I found quite hard to
o at first. I guess like
artist I wanted to stand
be unique, So when I
the life drawing Class I
ry even harder to be
. As I was drawing the
nd thinking I was doing
h my so called 'different'
e of the art tutors come
my drawing and then he
e picture up and down
n looking at me he said "Mmm,
e a bit of a Rembrandt!" Then he walked off.
... ed like I made a mistake. I'll give him

Got a name
for everything
you

Rembrandt I thought, so
took the picture down
and started again in
another style...
"Once again the sam
tutor came over w
the same manneri
and said "Mmm, that
like a Goya!" and th
walked off again.
Once again I changed
my style thinking this wi
throw him. Finally the
tutor come over and wa
looking real pleased wit
himself, then he said "Mm
I see a Leonardo!"
That's it I thought so I cu
and barked at him "have y
got a name for every fuck
drawing I do?" Guess I los
the plot there...
Nervously the tutor replie
"Sorry, calm down Glenn,
am paying your work c
compliment by comparin
it to other great artist!"
I felt stupid and flattere
to tell the truth I loved t
compliment and was hungr
for more, it changed my

I have to admit I was a bit like a mad dog when I started art school. To tell the truth, it was my insecure nature towards education that made me a little volatile. My experience of school did not give me the confidence I needed towards further education. I guess this could be put down to constantly being told I was thick by teachers. Eventually you end up believing it yourself...

To put this in a nutshell, I no longer wanted to be the subject of ridicule. After being exposed to war and becoming quite aware of my fighting ability, I swore to myself that I would no longer be mentally or physically bullied. Kind of the wrong attitude for further education, I know, but this attitude did give me the confidence to put my foot back in the door.

The educational environment was unlike anything that I had come to expect from school. For one, I was starting to get praise, something that I found quite hard to get used to at first. I guess like any other artist I wanted to stand out and be unique, so when I attended the life drawing class I would try even harder to be different. As I was drawing the model and thinking I was doing well with my so-called 'different' style, one of the art tutors came over to my drawing. He eyed the picture up and down and then looked at me. He said, "Mmm, looks like a bit of a Rembrandt." Then he walked off. This made me feel like I'd made a mistake. 'I'll give him Rembrandt,' I thought, so I took the picture down and started again in another style.

Once again the same tutor came over with the same mannerism and said, "Mmm, that's like a Goya," and then walked off. Once again I changed my style, thinking this would throw him. Finally the tutor came over and was looking real pleased with himself. Then he said, "Mmm, I see a Leonardo."

'That's it,' I thought, so I cut in and barked at him, "Have you got a name for every fucking drawing I do?" Guess I lost the plot there... Nervously, the tutor replied, "Sorry, calm down Glenn, I am paying your work a compliment by comparing it to other great artists." I felt stupid and flattered; to tell the truth, I loved the compliment and was hungry for more. It changed my attitude towards life and education.

I had just finished my lunch and was getting ready to settle the bill. All of a sudden a strange lady sat at my table and in a very well spoken voice asked me if she could talk to me, saying, "Please allow me to speak with you. I have been waiting for the chance. My guru sent me here to find you. It is important. He wants you to know."

I could not help thinking, 'Wierdo, I've got to listen to this one just for the comedy value.'

"Okay, go ahead," I said.

"Thank you," she said. "My guru sent me to tell you to stop using your powers so much. They could kill you. I know it sounds like a lot to take in but there is something cancerous in your head."

"O... k...," I said, not liking that. Then I thought, 'Think nothing of this looney, like she knows.'

"My guru is dead but he still talks to me. He also said you're an artist, a very good one," she said. I thought, 'Stalker, done your homework then.' "My name is Melanie. I am a clairvoyant and people usually come to see me. They pay £15 a session. My guru would not allow me to charge you. All he wants is to tell you is that you will be a famous artist if you channel your powers... Today I travelled from Ramsgate to find you. He told me you would be here. Thank you." Then she got up and left.

My powers? What did she mean?

PRESCIENT

just finished my lunch and was just getting ready to settle the bill
of a sudden a strange lady sat at my table and in a very well spoken voice
me if she could talk to me saying "Please allow me to speak with you, I have
the chance to speak with you, my guru sent me here to find you, it is important he
not help thinking weirdo, I got to listen to this one just for the comedy value "Ok, go
"Thankyou" she said, "My guru sent me to tell you to stop using your powers so much,
kill you. I know it sounds like alot to take in but there is something cancerous in
"O...k..." I said
Then I thought
this looney, like
"My Guru is
still talks to
said you're
very good one
I thought
your home
"My name
people usually
me, they pay
session. My
allow me to
all he wants is
is you will
artist if
Today I
Ramsgate
he told
be here,
Then she
left.
did she

Exposure
reat at University, I
fantastic new friends,
were going well, and we
tendency to drink like
as pretty much in my element.
king wow, if this is the
wonder what the second
like, bring it on:
ely for me when the
ar kicked in I started to
really bad headaches with
pains in the side of my head.
st put this
aving an
hangover
heory soon
the window
matter
did the
always
really got
t by this
ed to question
d anything to do with the
ns for chemical warfare that
ring the Gulf war, or even if
ything to do with handling
ed uranium rounds? I knew
was seriously wrong and
m needed medical
I just knew as I
to the doctor's this
THE GULF WAR DID NOT TAKE PLACE
RILLARD
The artistic guide to being brainwashed and indoctrinated to

Life was great at university. I had met fantastic new friends, my studies were going well and we all had a tendency to drink like fish so I was pretty much in my element. I kept thinking, 'Wow, if this is the first year, I wonder what the second one will be like: bring it on.'

Unfortunately for me when the second year kicked in, I started to develop really bad headaches with shooting pains in the side of my head. At first I just put this down to having an elongated hangover but that theory soon went out the window because no matter what I did the pain was always there.

I really got freaked out by this and started to question if this had anything to do with the inoculations for chemical warfare that we had during the Gulf War, or even if it had anything to do with handling the depleted uranium rounds.

I knew something was seriously wrong and this problem needed medical attention. I just knew as I walked into the doctor's that this would be the transition of my life.

If ever there was a dark period in my life, it had to be when I was 27. The relentless pain in my head was getting worse by the day; as to why, I didn't have a clue. The hardest thing at the time was trying to prove the pain in my head was not just a headache of imagination.

After I had been subjected to every type of headache pill under the sun, the doctors finally decided it was time to give me a brain scan. This came as a relief to me as I was beginning to lose faith in the system and wake up fearing for my life. I was asked if I was scared. Truth? "Yes, but I do not fear those trying to save my life..."

Somethings
Wrong
was a dark period in my life
when I was 27. The relentless
was getting worse by the day,
not have
ing at the
to prove
ache or
jected
nder
tors
it
is came
me as
o lose
SOMETHING
DARK
PERIOD

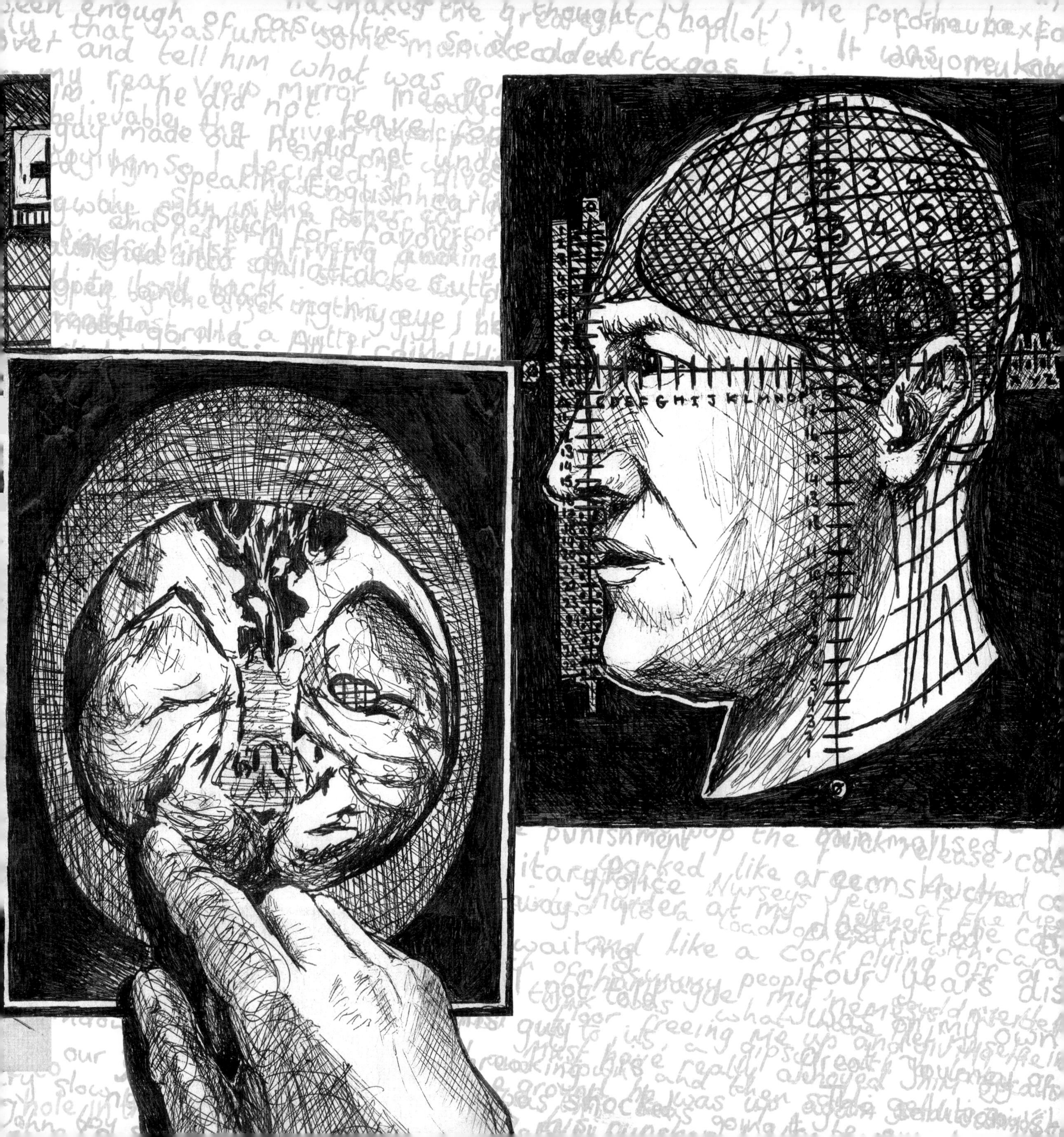

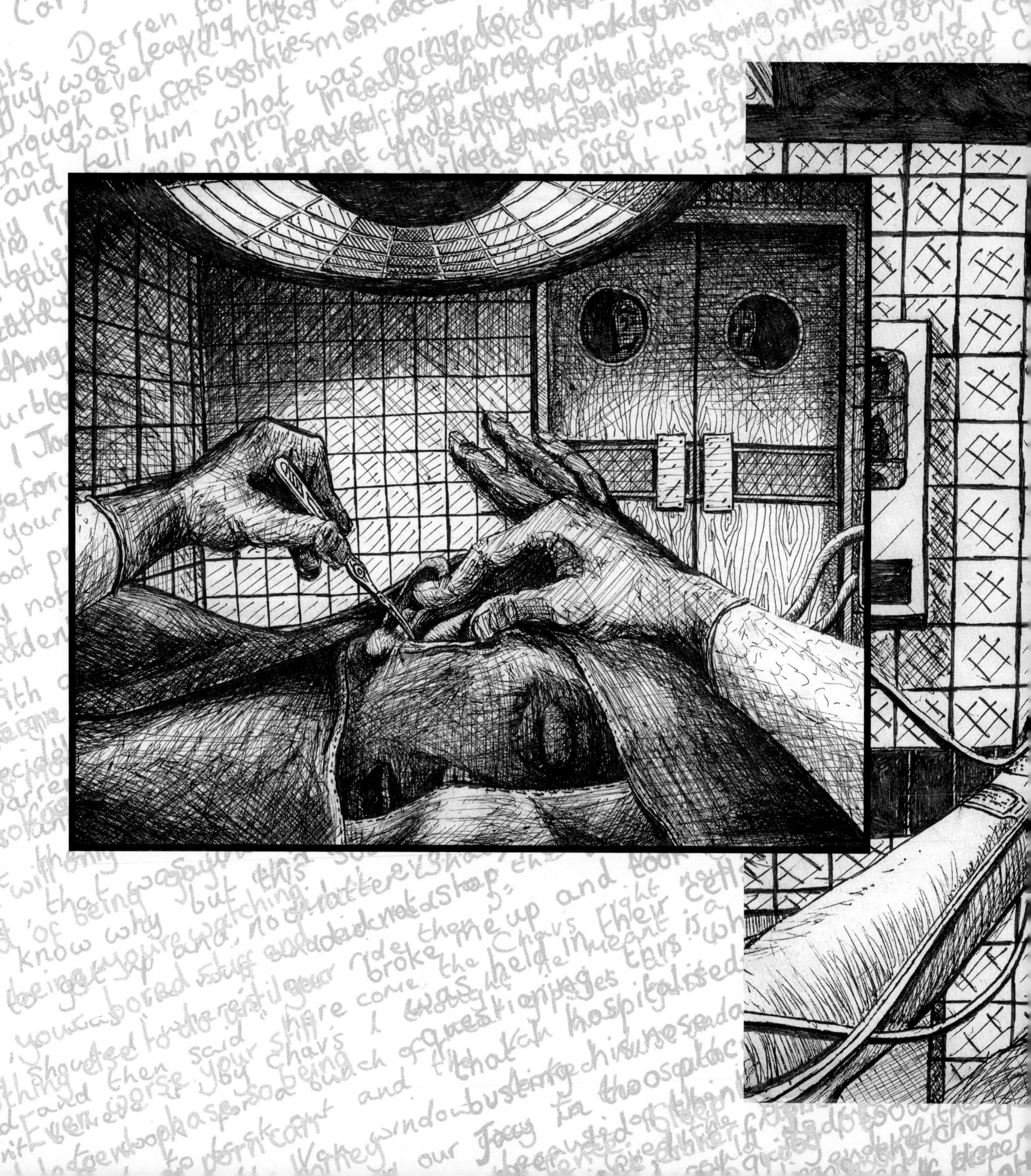

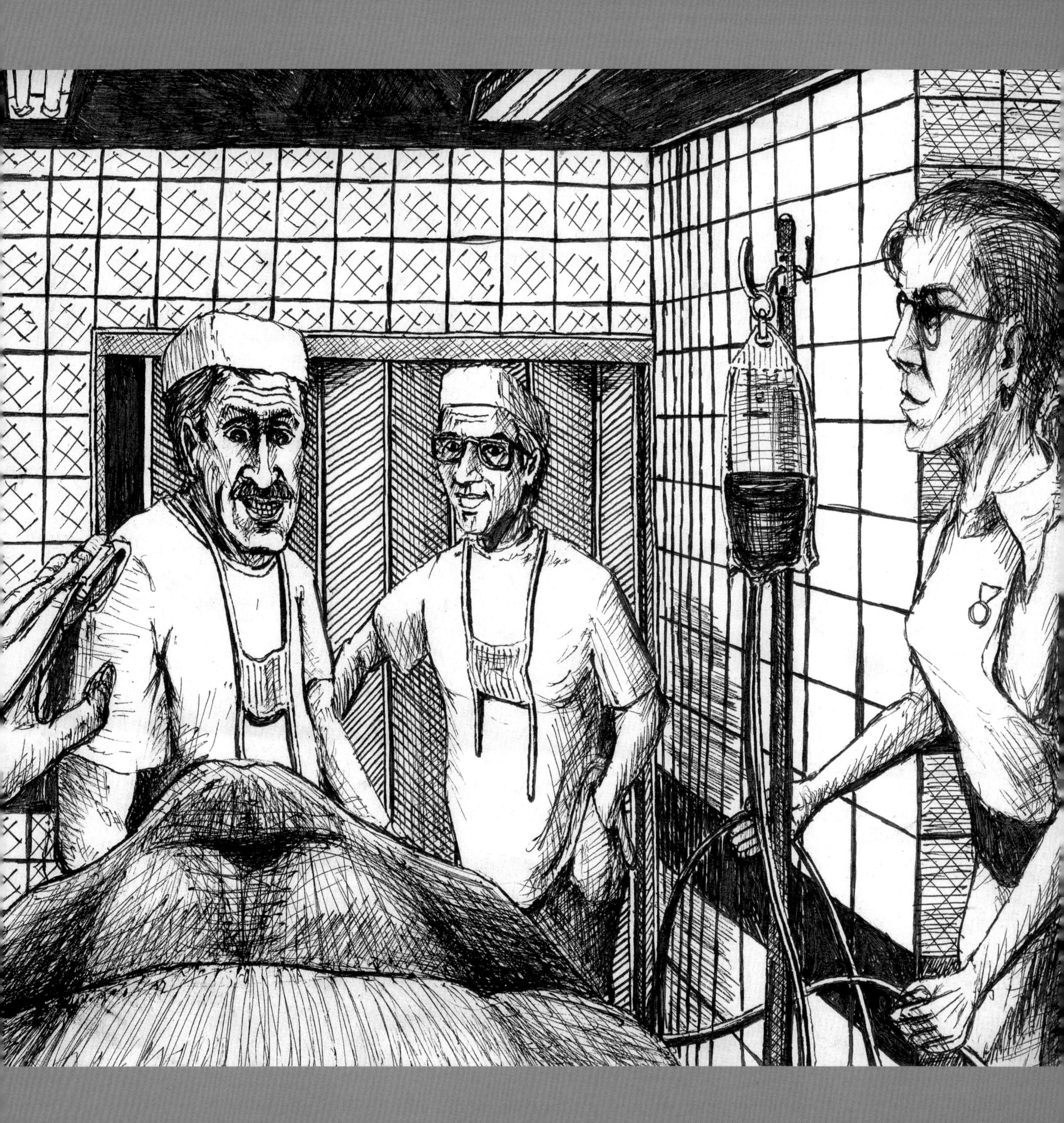

Nil
By
MOUTH

that was full of casualties some
er and tell him what was going
my rear view mirror
him if he did not leave
guy made out he did not understand
speaking English earlier
and so much for favours
into a boxing stance
lunatic to leave his attack wide
take off this brown Volvo driving
opportunity came and I seized it
a sign coming up rather
steering wheel
shot my punch straight through the
what the fucks going on
two Spanish guys jumped me
and was going for the kill
this sobered me up instantly I think it was
fight back
broke me up and took me away
I was held in their cells await
hospitalised this guy
to slow

As soon as I was fit enough, I went back to college. Although I did not really look the picture of health, I felt ready and raring to go. Knowing that I had just survived major surgery I felt like there was no stopping me now. It was great to get back and see all my friends again and they had me feeling very welcome upon arrival although in their eyes you could see the look of horror as they secretly stared at my swollen face and mega scar. I think this gave me the indication that my pulling days were over!

Okay, I admit I looked terrible. I still probably do now but to my surprise there was one woman, a real Belgian beauty, who could see past my scars and ended up going out with me. This really restored my confidence and for a pug ugly guy like me at the time I was going well and could not believe my luck.

Eventually Lin had to go home to Belgium and all I could think was, 'Oh well, it was good while it lasted.' Result: she wanted me to go over to Belgium to see her.

Wow, I had an open invitation and could not wait to see her again, so I saved my student loan and travelled over to Belgium for a lovely time.

SUPERFICIAL

n as I was fit enough I went back to college, although I did not really look the pict
lth I felt ready and raring to go. knowing I had Just survived major surgery I felt like
was no stopping me now. It was great to get back and see all my friends again and t
me feeling very welcome upon arrival although in their eyes you could see the look of ho
Secretly stared at my swollen face and mega scar, think this gave me the indication that
days were over? Ok I admit I looked terrible, I still probably do to date now and beyo
my surprise there was one woman a real Belgian beauty who could see passed my scars an
up going out with me. This really restored my confidence and for a pug ugly guy like me
e I was doing well and could not believe my luck.

lly Lin had to go
o Belgium and
uld think was
it was good
lasted.
e wanted
o over
um to
wow

n

1 WAY 2 HEAVEN

TISTO
DUVAL

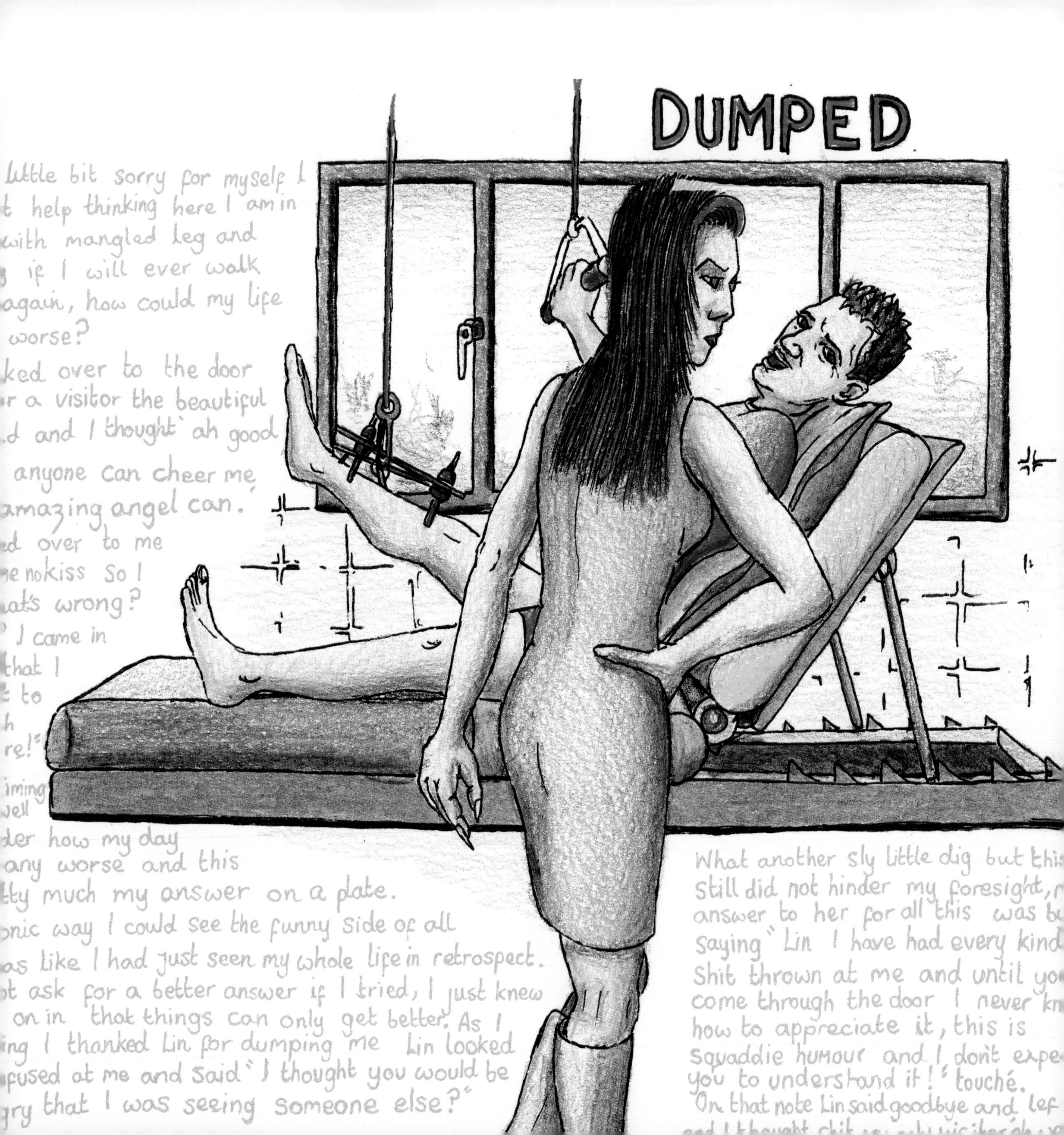
DUMPED
little bit sorry for myself I
t help thinking here I am in
with mangled leg and
g if I will ever walk
again, how could my life
worse?
ked over to the door
r a visitor the beautiful
d and I thought `ah good
anyone can cheer me
amazing angel can.'
ed over to me
ne no kiss so I
at's wrong?
I came in
that I
t to
h
re!'
iming
vell
der how my day
any worse and this
tty much my answer on a plate.
onic way I could see the funny side of all
as like I had just seen my whole life in retrospect.
ot ask for a better answer if I tried, I just knew
on in that things can only get better. As I
ing I thanked Lin for dumping me Lin looked
nfused at me and said `I thought you would be
gry that I was seeing someone else?'
What another sly little dig but this
still did not hinder my foresight,
answer to her for all this was b
saying `Lin I have had every kind
Shit thrown at me and until yo
come through the door I never kn
how to appreciate it, this is
squaddie humour and I don't expe
you to understand it!' touché.
On that note Lin said goodbye and lef

Feeling a little bit sorry for myself, I could not help thinking, 'Here I am in traction with mangled leg,' and wondering if I would ever walk properly again. How could my life get any worse?

As I looked over to the door hoping for a visitor, the beautiful Lin arrived and I thought, 'Ah, good timing, if anyone can cheer me up, this amazing angel can.' She walked over to me but this time, no kiss. So I asked, "What's wrong?" She said, "I came in to tell you that I don't want to go out with you any more."

Impeccable timing or what? Well, I did wonder how my day could get any worse and this was pretty much my answer on a plate.

In some ironic way, I could see the funny side of all this. It was like I had just seen my whole life in retrospect. I could not ask for a better answer if I tried. I just knew from here on in that things could only get better.

As I was laughing, I thanked Lin for dumping me. Lin looked really confused and said, "I thought you would be really angry that I was seeing someone else." Another sly little dig, but this still did not cloud my foresight. My answer to her for all this was by saying, "Lin, I have had every kind of shit thrown at me and until you came through the door, I never knew how to appreciate it. This is squaddie humour and I don't expect you to understand it." Touché. On that note, Lin said goodbye and left and I thought, 'Shit, my only visitor. Oh well...'

Being on crutches for an extremely long time made life pretty difficult no matter where you went, especially when it came to getting around on the London Underground trains.

I was having to make my way home after a squaddie reunion, so you can imagine I was pickled the night before. To add further insult to my injury, I was at the peak of my hangover, so this made it twice as difficult to get around on crutches. I had never travelled the Underground in that state before and this was going to prove quite an agonising experience.

My first obstacle to master was the escalator. It took me nearly 15 minutes to work out how to get on it with crutches. Although I was wearing the sympathy sticks, nobody offered me a hand (typical of the rush hour subculture). As soon as I got on the escalator, I realised I would have to get off; there was no choice and only one chance because this escalator was not going to stop for me. Before I knew it, I'd arrived at the bottom of the moving stairs and had to make an untimely jump towards the static ground. This made me take a tumble, hitting the ground like a sack of spuds. And still the subculture stepped around me.

Finally I made it to the train and was able to sit down at last. Home was on my horizon; that was until I fell asleep and was woken up in Uxbridge, about 50 stops more than I needed. I had to change trains and start the journey over again. Silly me, I fell asleep once more and then woke up back in Uxbridge. It was the longest day of my life.

Advice: If you're ever offered a lift home, don't stay for another beer, take the lift!

UXBRIDGE

on crutches for an extremely long time made life pretty difficult no matter where you wer
ially when it came to getting around on the London underground trains.
s having to make my way home after being at a squaddie reunion, so you can imagine I was p
night before. To add further insult to my injury
s at the peak of my hangover, so this made
ice as difficult to get around on crutches.
never travelled the underground in that
before and this was going to prove
to be quite an agonizing
ience.
st obstacle
ster was
scalator, this
took me
inutes to
out how
on it with
ches, although
wearing the
thy sticks
y offered me
d (typical of
sh hour
lture).
on as I got on the
tor I realized
d have to get
there was no
and only
ance to get
cause this
or was not
o stop for
Before I knew

bottom of the moving stairs and I
make an untimely jump toward
static ground, this made
take a turn
hitting the g
like a sack o
and still the
subculture st
around me.
Finally I made
the train and
able to sit d
last, home wa
horizon, that
until I fell a
and was w
in Uxbridge
fifty stops more than
needed. I had to
trains and start t
journey over a
Silly me I fell a
again and t
woke up in
again, it w
the longest
my life.
Advice, if you
offered a lift
don't stay for

There is light at the end of the tunnel

and eventual
you find it a
at the end o
and eventual
light at the e
tunnel and e
find it at the e
the end of t
and eventual
there is light

and eventually you will find it.

Finally it was my end of year MA (Master of Arts) show, a time to exhibit art, hopefully selling it and celebrating. The show was good and at the time the drink was even better. Some drinking games were taking place and even the landlord of my local pub was getting the taste. Afterwards we went to our local and had a lock-in until the early hours of the morning.

After nearly drinking the pub dry, the four of us literally fell out of the pub door and headed toward home. En route we could not help noticing a lone Morris Minor. I don't know why but as soon as we saw it we burst into fits of laughter.

Don't know why again, but as my friend Rich was laughing, he said, "Did you know you can get them cars open with your front door key?"

"Yeah right," I replied in a sarcastic manner, almost egging him on to do it. So he did, and even worse, we all got in the car for a quick sit down.

After about five minutes of sitting and doing nothing, we all decided to get out and go home. Someone even suggested when we got out we lock it just in case someone stole it, so we did. Just as we locked the car, the police arrived and rushed us. They roughed us up a bit and then handcuffed us. They bundled us into their van and took us to their station. They locked us up for 18 hours. I remember waking up in the cell thinking, 'What a night.'

Rich and I had to go to court. We went twice because the magistrate did not know what to charge us with. In the end he made us apologise and promise not to do it again. Then he had us thrown out of court.

MINOR OFFENCE
d of year M.A. (Master of Arts) show, a time to exhibit art,
l celebrating. The show was good and at the time the drink was even better. Some
taking place and even the landlord of my local pub was getting the taste. After we
had a lock in until the early hours of the morning.
the pub dry the four of us literally fell out of the pub door and headed towards home.
help noticing a lone Morris Minor, l
s Soon as we see it we burst into
OLD CITY BA
n but as
ughing
ou
en
he
wn.
s of
ing
out
even
t out
se
we did.
he car the
rushed us.
bit and then hand-cuffed
Rich and I had to go to court,
we went twice because the
magistrate did not know
what to charge us with.

THE CIDER CYCLE
Momentum is what you need when you're drink cycling. I didn't think it would any harm If I rode my
ome in my drunken state. I know, I should have known better after being done for drink driving (which
none tooproud of), however I took to resorting back to the old trusty bicycle as a means
f transport, a good solution for getting around cheaply (taxi avoiding). I admit I was
obbly on the bike,
ut I felt fine
nd as long as I
as travelling
orward without
topping I would
ave no problem
aking all the way
ome...
Sozzled
hat was until I got pulled over by the police, then the nightmare of
aving to stop began. As soon as I stopped, I forgot to put my feet on
he ground, before I knew it, I tilted sideways and fell through the
ence with my bike still attatched to me. As I got back up the W.P.C was
rying her hardest not to laugh at me. The policeman wasn't amused so he gave me a right tellin
 it wasn't for the giggling W.P.C. I would have been done again. I was told to walk the bike home after tha

Momentum is what you need when you've drunk cider. I didn't think it would do any harm if I rode my bike home in my drunken state. I know, I should have known better after being done for drink driving (which I am none too proud of). However, I took to resorting back to the old trusty bicycle as a means of transport, a good solution for getting around cheaply (avoiding taxi).

I admit I was wobbly on the bike, but I felt fine and as long as I was travelling forward without stopping, I would have no problem making it all the way home...

That was until I got pulled over by the police. Then the nightmare of having to stop began. As I stopped, I forgot to put my feet on the ground. I tilted sideways and fell through the fence with my bike still attached to me. As I got back up the WPC was trying her hardest not to laugh. The policeman wasn't amused so he gave me a right telling off. It it wasn't for the giggling WPC, I would have been done again. I was told to walk the bike home after that.

After having a great time in the nightclub where Boz and I got completely drunk, Boz took it upon himself to fall over backwards and split his head open on the curb, therefore requiring hospital attention (selfish git, I wanted to get home early that night). Somehow we miraculously got a lift to the hospital from some random crazy driver who, once we were in motion, told us he was more pissed than the two of us put together. How we ended up getting a lift from this guy I guess I will never know.

Anyway, after the nightmare lift from hell, we reached the hospital in one piece only to discover two discarded wheelchairs at the hospital entrance. For Boz and me it was too hard to resist playing 'Days of Thunder' and having a wheelchair race, which went horribly wrong due to going downhill too fast and not being able to stop the inertia for fear of getting skin-burned hands off the wheels and having an accident, which we did, by crashing into each other at the bottom of the hill. It was only just after that we discovered wheelchairs have brakes.

After the great wheelchair race and being told off for it, two girls asked if they could sit with us. They were quite pretty, including the one with blood all over her face who looked like she had just played the lead in the film 'Carrie'. They'd noticed our comedy value; that's all we had going for us. It killed time.

We were all having a good laugh, that was until I noticed Boz snogging Bloodhead. Even her friend pointed at the two blood-covered lovers, saying, "That's disgusting." Next they went outside for a bit more.

After about 20 minutes, Boz and Bloodhead came back hand in hand. Boz had the biggest grin I have ever seen. I asked if he had given her one. He replied, giggling and waving his blood-covered hand in front of me, "No, but at least I got one clean finger out of it!" QED.

SLIPSTREAMING

a great time in the night club where Boz and I got completely drunk, Boz took it upon
all over backwards and split his head open on the curb therefore requiring hospital attention (selfish
to get home early that night). Somehow we miraculously got a lift to the hospital from some random crazy
ce we were in motion, told us he was more pissed than the two of us put together, how we ended getting
's guy I guess I will never know. Anyway after the nightmare lift from hell we reached the hospital in one
o discover two discarded wheel chairs at the hospital entrance, for Boz and I it was too hard
ing 'Days of Thunder' and having a wheel chair race, which went horribly wrong due to going
fast and not being able to stop the inertia for the fear of getting skin burnt hands off
and having an accident, which we did, by crashing into each other at the bottom of the
only just after that we discovered wheel chairs
.
t wheel chair race and being told off for it
e pretty including the one
over her face
ke she had
the lead in
rrie', asked if
t with us after
comedy value,
d going for us.
and we were all
d laugh, that was
d Boz snogging
even her
d at the
ered

After about 20 minutes
Boz and Bloodhead
came back hand
in hand, Boz had the
biggest grin I had ever
seen. I asked Boz
if he gave her one
he replied giggling
and waving his blood
hand infront of me
'No, but at least
I got one clean
finger out of
it!'

MANNERS COST NOTHING

ess it would be fair to say I have been the unrewarded Jack of all trades and master of n
ve even tried my hand at being a karaoke D.J. for the local night club, unfortunately for me m
ened to coincide with the golden oldies' night, this was the night that attracted all the lo
eed nutters. It was almost heart breaking thinking you were only trying to provide a good time f
yone and only to be told by the local knuckle dragging looney to put them on next or meet y
l after the night was over, it never happened because these type of people had the memory of
fish and would disappear into the crowd wondering why their song had not been played

To tell the truth, this career move was s
lived because I don't do rude and coul
help myself from wanting to terminate th
I would still love to catch up with
those who
threatened me
you never
know.
Oi, I'm next or I will see you later
Oh please die now
ALL BY MYSELF
Didn't know her name but she used to pick the knickers out of her arse every week.
Sexy...

I guess it would be fair to say I have been the unrewarded jack of all trades and master of none. I have even tried my hand at being a karaoke DJ for the local nightclub. Unfortunately for me, my slot happened to coincide with the golden oldies' night. This was the night that attracted all the local inbred nutters. It was almost heart breaking, thinking you were only trying to provide a good time for everyone only to be told by the local knuckle dragging loony to put them on next or meet your peril after the night was over. It never happened because this type of person had the memory of a goldfish and would disappear into the crowd wondering why their song had not been played next.

To tell the truth, this career move was short-lived because I don't do rude and could not help myself from wanting to terminate this breed. I would still love to catch up with those who threatened me, you never know.

(I didn't know her name but she used to pick the knickers out of her arse every week. Sexy...)

There came a time in my life where I could see no light at the end of the tunnel. It was like all the major events of my life had caught up as soon as I finished art school. I was very much afraid of going back into the real world. I could not help worrying about the head surgery, being run over and having my leg broken, the stress of the Gulf War and my leaving the security blanket of being at art school. I knew after all this I was not the total fit person I used to be. I really wanted to hide from the world because of all that. I could not help thinking that in my condition, I would be of no use to anyone because I was no longer A1 fit. I felt more like I would be a liability in the eyes of any employer. Basically this had me at an all-time low in self-esteem.

I felt very much alone. I had lost contact with all my friends in the Army, people who I had trusted with my life. Everyone else at art school had disappeared back home or were already set up. As much as I have great loving parents, there really was no room at home for me because it was a full house as my brothers and sisters were still living there.

Thanks to some friends who put me up here and there, I was just able to keep from being homeless. It was time to seek help. I am grateful to my local doctor, the British Legion and the War Veterans Association who managed to put me on the right track by introducing me to a place called Tyrwhitt House, a combat stress centre that dealt with a whole variety of problems for the ex-serviceman.

This place really came to my rescue and even more so the people and comrades who I met there. We were all on common ground and could laugh and cry at our experiences. Just knowing I had somewhere to turn in times of trouble gave me a fresh start and a light at the end of the tunnel.

TYRWHITT HOUSE

time in my life where I could see no light at the end of the tunnel, it was like all the major
ce had caught me up as soon as I finished art school. I was very much afraid of goin
real world, I could not help worring about the head surgery, the being run over and
roken, the
e war and
ecurity
t art
ter all
he
used
wanted
world
t, I
inking
would be
one
longer
re
es
me
ery low self
one, I had lost
y friends in the
I had trusted
one else at at art school
back home or were already set up for life.
great loving parents, there really was no
r me because it was a full house
and sisters were still living there.

With great
thanks to
some friend
who put m
up here and
there, I was
just able to k
from being
homele
It was
time to
seek he
and with
many than
to my local
doctor, the
British legion
and the Wa
veterans
association, the
managed to put m
on the right track
by introducing me
to a place called
Tyrwitt House, a
Combat stress centr
This place dealt with
a whole variety of problems fo
the ex-servicemen.

This place really came to my rescue and even
more so the people and comrades who I met there
We were all on common grounds and could laugh
and cry at our experiences, just knowing I had
somewhere to turn to in times of trouble gave me a
fresh start again, and a light at the end of the tunnel.

The Future Is Bright
meet some real interesting people in life
nd ex-military man who had done active
fered injuries due to an explosion.
has had all the troubles of the world
kes me realize there are no concessions
I could not believe it when he told
in front of a War pensions committee
up and down on a small box.
emed him fit and reduced his pension
ear about this, It made me
doing that and thinking is that
if I am lucky enough to live that
admired about Tom was his spirit,
mile and refused to let these
ers beat him down. It was the
k to the tribunal that really made it
am an 86 year old man and have
life with out you lot breathing
an't take much more of this!"
y he stuck his two fingers
and said " Here,
your arse, I'm off to
bout you lot!" Then he
stir amongst the panel
ne to fetch Tom back, they
hat one so they said they
Situation:
you really have to put up with that.

Sometimes you meet some really interesting people in life, like Tom Burgess, 86 and an ex-military man who had done active service and had suffered injuries from an explosion. This is someone who has had all the troubles of the world thrust upon him. It makes me realise there are no concessions even at the age of 86.

I could not believe it when he told me he had had to stand in front of a War Pensions committee and was made to step up and down on a small box. To his horror, they deemed him fit and reduced his pension. I was disgusted to hear about this. It made me picture myself at 86 doing that and thinking, 'Is that what I will be doing if I am lucky enough to live that long?'

One thing I really admired about Tom was his spirit. He still managed to smile and refused to let these pension penny pinchers beat him down. It was the way he answered back to the tribunal that really made it for me. He said, "I am an 86 year old man and have had a hard enough life without you lot breathing down my neck. I can't take much more of this." In a Milliganesque way, he stuck his two fingers up at the committee and said, "Here, stick my pension up your arse. I'm off to tell the Daily Mail about you lot!" Then he stormed off.

This caused quite a stir among the panel, so they sent someone to fetch Tom back. They were worried about that one so they said they would review Tom's situation.

Really, at 86, should you have to put up with that?

I must really take the biscuit for beng asked to do random jobs. I was asked if I wanted to earn some extra cash by working at the nightclub on Christmas Eve. I wasn't in a position to turn it down because I was broke. I noticed the person who was with my boss at the time kept looking and giggling at me. I wondered why. The penny dropped after I was told I would have to dress up as Father Christmas that night. "Sounds all right," I said. On gay night, probably not such as good idea. Why is there always a catch when I am asked to do something**?**

Even worse for me, there was a grotto specially built for the occasion with a big chair in it. My job now was to let the customers - men, women, gay, straight - come into the grotto, sit on my knee and tell me what they wanted for Christmas. That night I heard and met all sorts. There were even two boys who sat on my knees and started bitch fighting because one pointed at the other, saying, "Santa, my boyfriend there needs a bigger cock for Christmas."

It sure was an interesting night. Some random girl even offered to give me a blow job. So I let her, but she said, "One condition: if I do, you keep the beard on. I don't want to know who you are."

Best night's work I have ever done and been paid for.

CHRISTMAS CUM EARLY

st really take the biscuit for being asked to do random Jobs. I was asked if I wanted to earn some extra h by working at the night club Christmas eve , I wasn't in the position to turn it down because I was broke. ticed the person who was with my boss at the time kept looking and giggling at me, I wondered why. The ny dropped after I was told I would have to dress up as father Christmas that night, sounds alright, on gay night bably not and why is there always a catch when I am asked to do something? Even worse for me there was grotto with a big chair in it especially built for the occasion, my job now was to the customers, men, women y or straight come into the grotto, sit on my knee and let them tell me what they want for Christmas! t night I heard and met all sorts, there was even two boys that sat on my knees and started bitch fighting cause one pointed at the other saying "Santa, my boyfriend ere needs a bigger k for Christmas!"

It sure was an interesting night, even some random girl offered to give me a blow Job.

Ho Ho Hoooyeahh

So I let her, but she said" One condition if I do, you keep the beard on, I don't want to know who you are!"

Best night's work I have ever done and been Paid for.

ALMOST
When having been asked why didn't we fini
the job in Iraq and remove Saddam from po
I can only answer I don't really know myself
Our main objective was to liberate Kuwait a
that's what we did, basically we won our o
I always believed, along with so many other m
out there, we as a peace keeping force sho
have removed the evil dictator and the ti
was perfect, we was close enough to Bagd
and ready for extraction. What was the poi
liberating Kuwait and saying "don't do it again Sa
This no one could e
fathom, here you
a meglomaniac
our leaders rea
think given tim
he would be
to do busines
with?
Unfortunatel
seemed the
time to pull t
plu
Ta
th
Cap
an
ru
GULF
OiL
GAME OVER
WARS
OIL
Q8

When I have been asked why we didn't finish the job in Iraq and remove Saddam from power, I can only answer, "I don't really know myself." Our main objective was to liberate Kuwait and that's what we did; basically we won our oil.

I have always believed, along with so many other men out there, that we as a peace-keeping force should have removed the evil dictator. The time was perfect; we were close enough to Baghdad and ready for extraction. What was the point of liberating Kuwait and saying, "Don't do it again, Saddam!" This no one could even fathom. Here you have a megalomaniac. Did our leaders really think, given time, he would be good to do business with?

Unfortunately it seemed the right time to pull the plug. Take the capital and run.

On reflection, self evolution can be a very funny thing. We all have a personal journey to get through but like any great journey in life, you can be ill-equipped if you don't have any confidence and self belief (two very hard traits to come by but achievable with the right guidelines).

I may have started life on the wrong foot – basically a chav with a lost soul and no real sense of direction – but deep down my heart kept pushing me in the direction of art. I admit in my earlier days I lacked confidence and didn't really know how to stand up and be counted, leading me to hide from one of the only talents I have. It was only experience and many diverse situations that kicked me up the arse and pushed me back into art.

And I love it. Once I had accepted myself and the environment around me, I felt ready to evolve and move on. Breaking my old mould made an opening to put my foot in the door.

Having the opportunity to do art has been my salvation: never deny creativity no matter what form it may come in. Once I realised I could express myself and reach out and take advice (at last), I also realised I had become a much better person for it. I just hope from here on in I can touch hearts and continue to entertain people with the art that I lay before them...